A TREASURY OF XXth CENTURY MURDER

# Black Dahlia

nbm GRAPHIC
NOVELS

Nantier · Beall · Minoustchine
N E W

Rick Geary was born in 1946 in Kansas City, Missouri and grew up in Wichita, Kansas. He graduated from the University of Kansas in Lawrence, where his first cartoons were published in the University Daily Kansan.

He worked as staff artist for two weekly papers in Wichita before moving to San Diego in 1975.

He began work in comics in 1977 and was for thirteen years a contributor to the Funny Pages of National Lampoon. His comic stories have also been published in Heavy Metal, Dark Horse Comics and the DC Comics/ Paradox Press Big Books.

During a four-year stay in New York, his illustrations appeared regularly in The New York Times Book Review. His illustration work has also been seen in MAD, Spy, Rolling Stone, The Los Angeles Times, and American Libraries.

He has written and illustrated three children's books based on The Mask for Dark Horse and two Spider-Man children's books for Marvel. His children's comic Society of Horrors ran in Disney Adventures magazine from 1999 to 2006. He's also done comics for Gumby.

In 1989, he started the multi-volume true crime, highly acclaimed series Treasury of Murder with NBM Graphic Novels for which he is mostly known today.

In 2007, after more than thirty years in San Diego, he and his wife Deborah moved to the town of Carrizozo, New Mexico.

Also available wherever e-books are sold

ISBN: 978-1-68112-178-9

1st paperback printing December 2018

# BLACK Dahlia !

WRITTEN AND ILLUSTRATED by

**Rick GEAry**

**Also available by Geary:**
**A Treasury of Victorian Murder:**
Vol. I, pb., E-book
Jack The Ripper, pb., E-book
The Borden Tragedy, pb.
The Fatal Bullet, pb, E-book
The Mystery of Mary Rogers, pb., E-book
The Beast of Chicago, pb., E-book
The Murder of Abraham Lincoln, pb., hc., E-book
The Bloody Benders, pb., E-book
The Case of Madeleine Smith, pb., hc.
A Treasury of Victorian Murder Compendium I, pb.
A Treasury of Victorian Murder Compendium II, hc.
**A Treasury of XXth Century Murder:**
The Lindbergh Child, pb.,E-book
Famous Players, pb., hc., E-book
The Axe-Man of New Orleans, hc., pb., E-book
The Lives of Sacco & Vanzetti, pb., E-book
Lovers Lane, hc., E-book
Madison Square Tragedy, hc., E-book
Black Dahlia, pb., E-book
A Treasury of XXth Century Murder Compendium I, hc.
**Fiction:**
Louise Brooks, Detective, hc., E-book
**Biography:**
The True Death of Billy the Kid, hc., E-book

**see more on these and order at our website:**
**nbmpub.com**

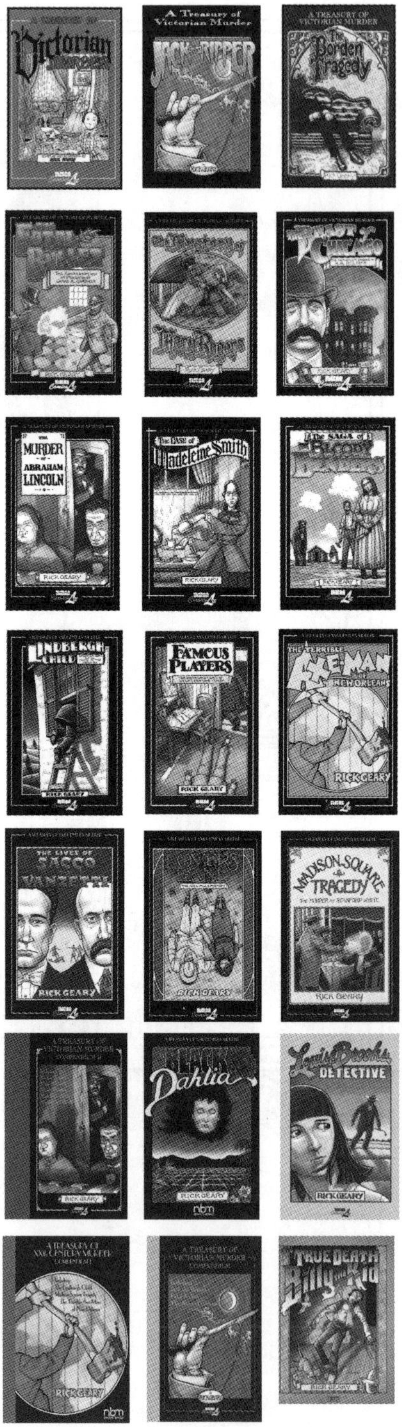

We have over 200 titles
Catalog available upon request
NBM
160 Broadway, Suite 700, East Wing,
New York, NY 10038

# BLACK DAHLIA
# BIBLIOGRAPHY

Gilmore, John, *Severed: The True Story of the Black Dahlia*.
(Los Angeles, Amok Books, 2006)

Douglas, John and Mark Olshaker, *The Cases That Haunt Us*.
(New York, Scribner, 2000)

Hodel, Steve, *Black Dahlia Avenger*.
(New York, Arcade Publishing, 2003)

Wolfe, Donald H., *The Black Dahlia Files*.
(New York, Regan Books, 2006)

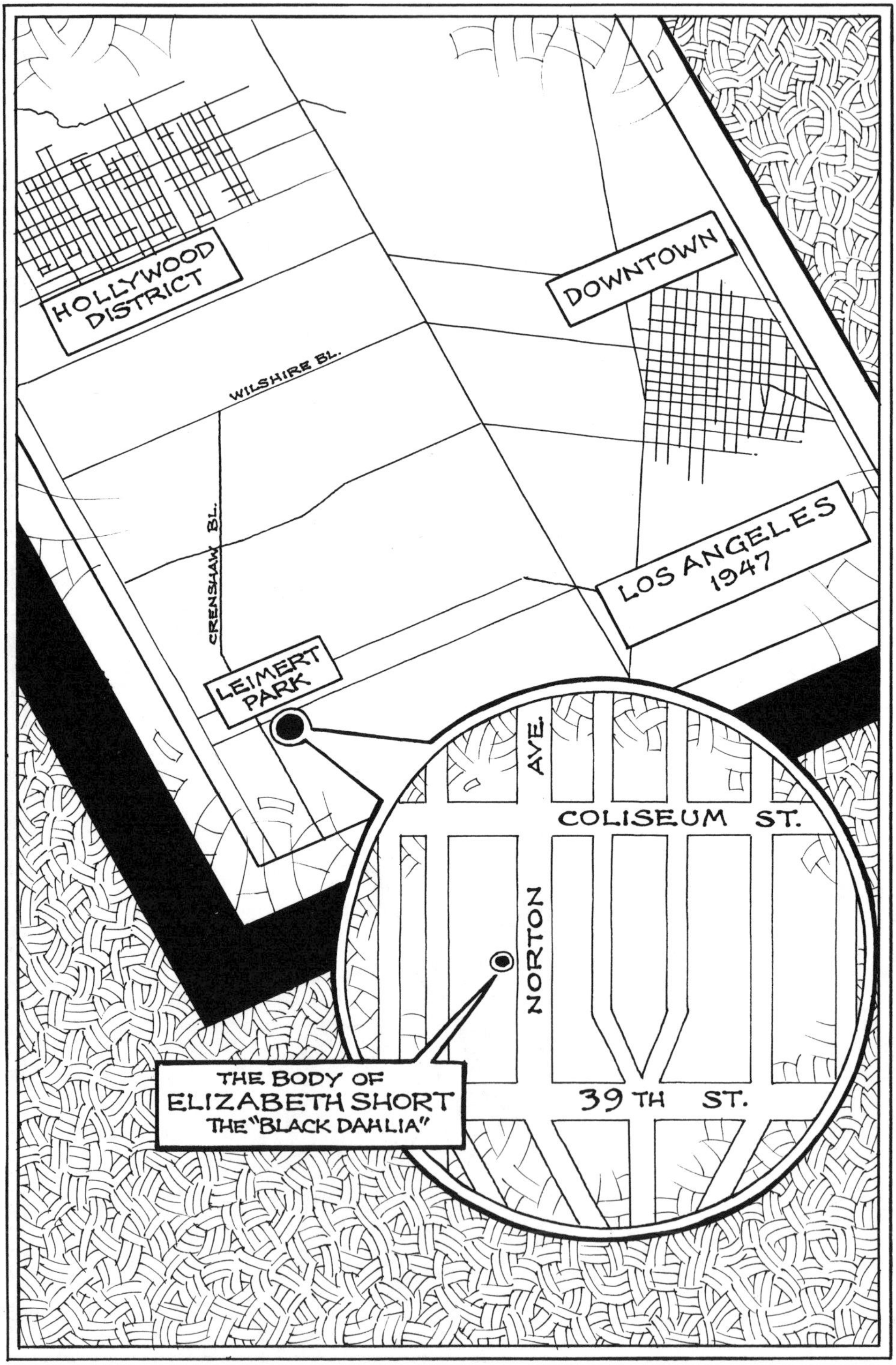
HOLLYWOOD DISTRICT
WILSHIRE BL.
DOWNTOWN
CRENSHAW BL.
LOS ANGELES 1947
LEIMERT PARK
AVE.
COLISEUM ST.
NORTON
39 TH ST.
THE BODY OF ELIZABETH SHORT THE "BLACK DAHLIA"

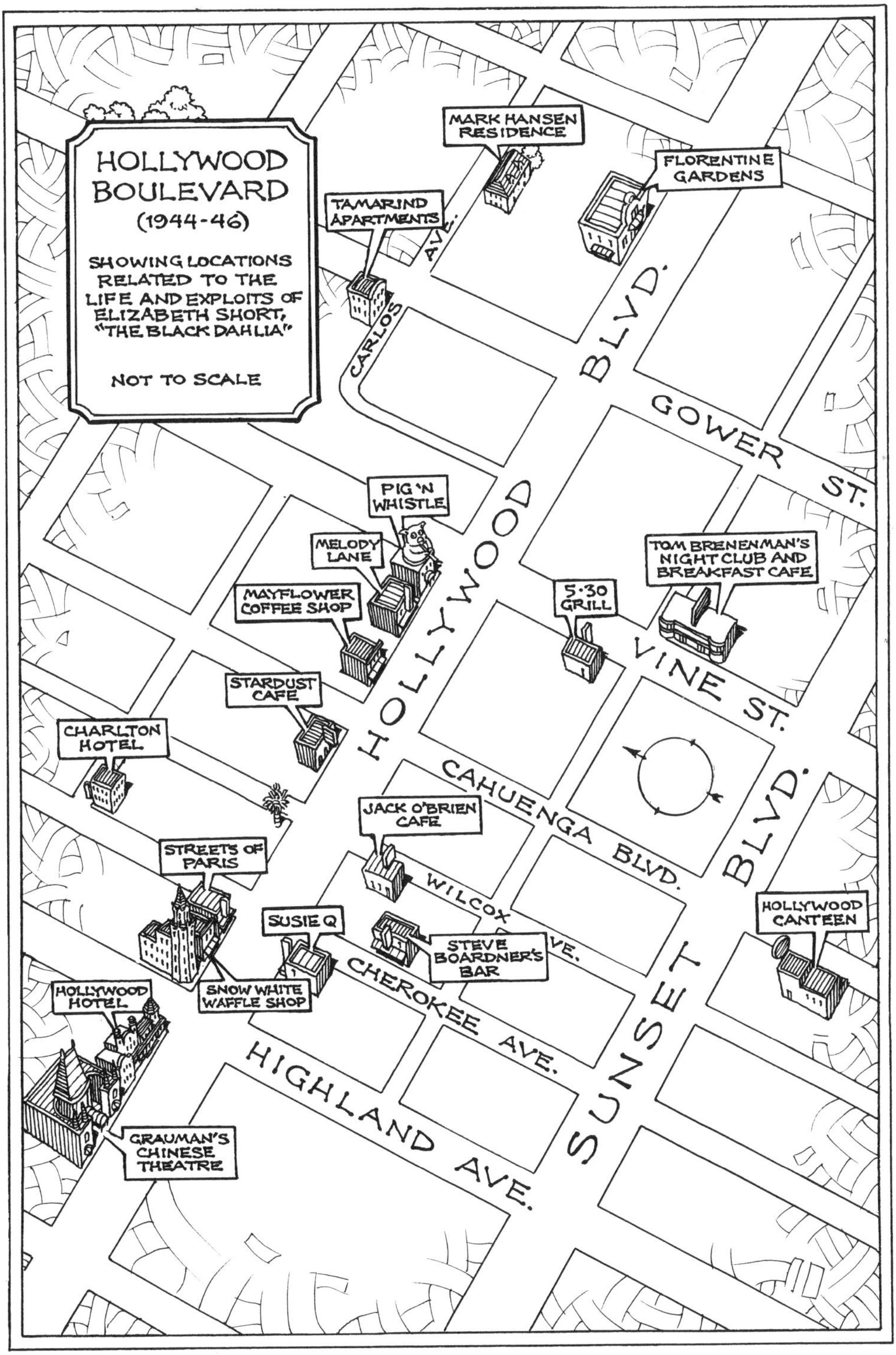

HOLLYWOOD BOULEVARD
(1944-46)
SHOWING LOCATIONS RELATED TO THE LIFE AND EXPLOITS OF ELIZABETH SHORT, "THE BLACK DAHLIA"
NOT TO SCALE
MARK HANSEN RESIDENCE
FLORENTINE GARDENS
TAMARIND APARTMENTS
CARLOS AVE.
HOLLYWOOD BLVD.
GOWER ST.
PIG 'N WHISTLE
MELODY LANE
MAYFLOWER COFFEE SHOP
TOM BRENENMAN'S NIGHT CLUB AND BREAKFAST CAFE
5·30 GRILL
VINE ST.
STARDUST CAFE
CHARLTON HOTEL
CAHUENGA BLVD.
JACK O'BRIEN CAFE
STREETS OF PARIS
WILCOX AVE.
SUSIE Q
STEVE BOARDNER'S BAR
HOLLYWOOD CANTEEN
SNOW WHITE WAFFLE SHOP
CHEROKEE AVE.
HOLLYWOOD HOTEL
SUNSET BLVD.
HIGHLAND AVE.
GRAUMAN'S CHINESE THEATRE

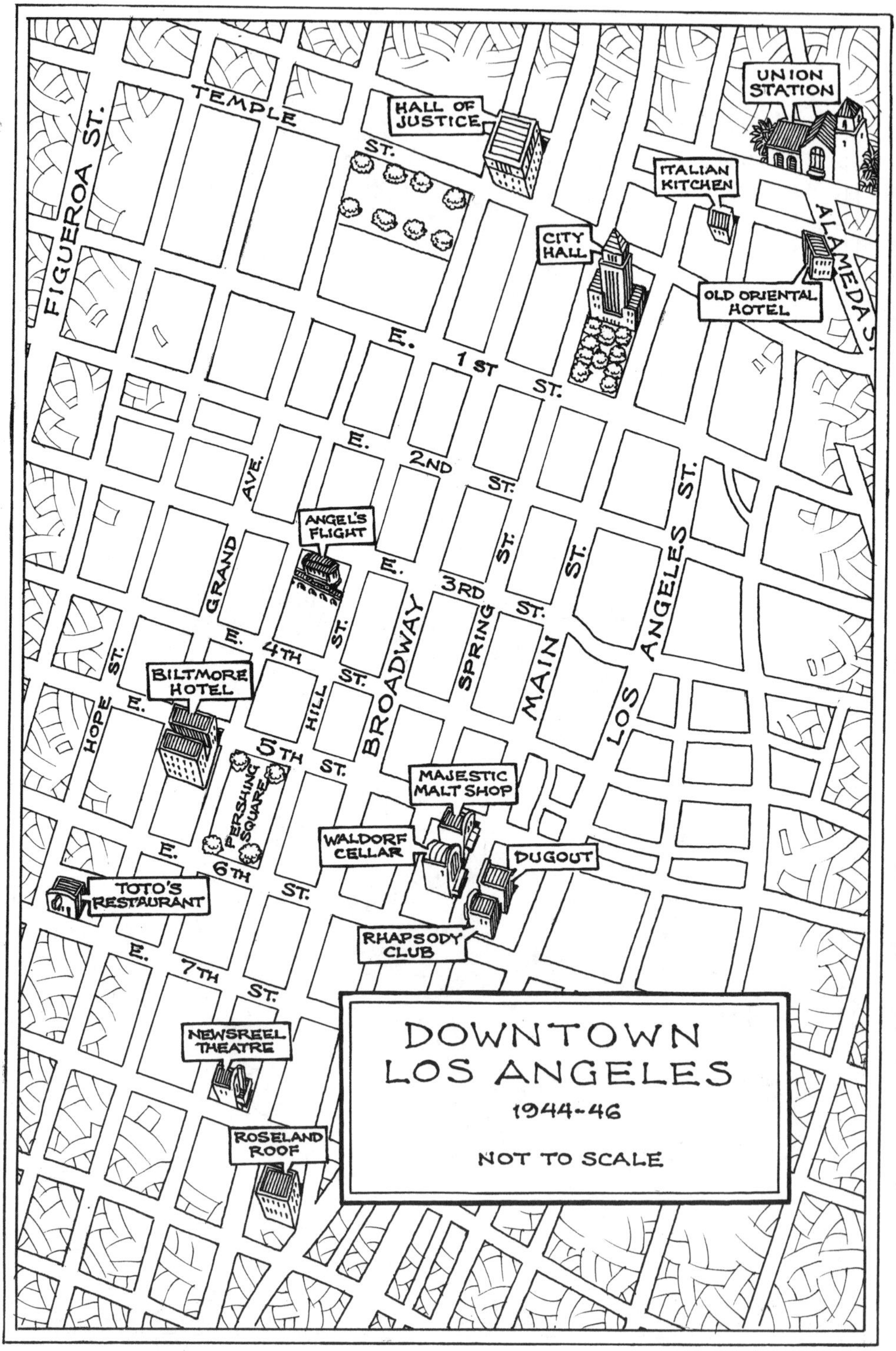
DOWNTOWN
LOS ANGELES
1944-46
NOT TO SCALE
UNION STATION
HALL OF JUSTICE
TEMPLE ST.
FIGUEROA ST.
ITALIAN KITCHEN
CITY HALL
OLD ORIENTAL HOTEL
ALAMEDA ST.
E. 1ST ST.
E. 2ND ST.
E. 3RD ST.
E. 4TH ST.
E. 5TH ST.
E. 6TH ST.
E. 7TH ST.
GRAND AVE.
ANGEL'S FLIGHT
SPRING ST.
MAIN ST.
LOS ANGELES ST.
HOPE ST.
HILL ST.
BROADWAY
BILTMORE HOTEL
PERSHING SQUARE
MAJESTIC MALT SHOP
WALDORF CELLAR
DUGOUT
TOTO'S RESTAURANT
RHAPSODY CLUB
NEWSREEL THEATRE
ROSELAND ROOF

# PART ONE

# THE VACANT LOT

LOS ANGELES, CALIFORNIA
1947

THE WAR IS OVER, AND THE CITY OF SUN-WASHED DREAMS
STRUGGLES TO REGAIN ITS NORMAL FOOTING...
NEVER IMAGINING WHAT HORROR AWAITS ON A CRISP,
OVERCAST WINTER MORNING.

WEDNESDAY, JANUARY 15, 1947

AT ABOUT 10:00AM, MRS. BETTY BERSINGER WALKS WITH HER 3-YEAR-OLD DAUGHTER IN THE LEIMERT PARK NEIGHBORHOOD EAST OF DOWNTOWN.

THEY ARE MAKING THEIR WAY ALONG A VACANT LOT ON NORTON AVE. BETWEEN COLISEUM AND 39TH STREETS, WHEN THE LADY SPIES A WHITE FIGURE RECUMBENT ON THE GROUND.

AT FIRST, IT APPEARS TO BE A DEPARTMENT STORE MANNIKIN, DISCARDED INTO THE WEEDS... IN TWO SECTIONS.

A CLOSER LOOK SHOWS IT TO BE THE BODY OF A YOUNG WOMAN...

GROTESQUELY POSED...

HIDEOUSLY MUTILATED...

AND NEATLY CUT IN HALF AT THE WAIST.

MRS. BERSINGER LETS OUT A SCREAM AND RUNS TO THE NEAREST HOUSE.

THERE SHE CALLS THE POLICE.

THE DISPATCHER AT UNIVERSITY STATION CALLS OUT A 390: A "MAN DOWN."

BUT BEFORE A UNIT CAN RESPOND, THE CALL IS INTERCEPTED BY TWO MEMBERS OF THE PRESS:

WILL FOWLER OF THE LOS ANGELES EXAMINER AND A PHOTOGRAPHER, FELIX PAGEL.

THEY RECORD THE SCENE PAINSTAKINGLY.

EVEN IN ORDINARY CIRCUMSTANCES, THE CITY'S SIX DAILY NEWSPAPERS ENGAGE IN A DEADLY COMPETITION.

BUT IT IS HEARST'S AFTERNOON EXAMINER AND ITS MORNING COUNTERPART, THE HERALD EXPRESS, THAT WILL REMAIN AT THE CENTER OF THIS SENSATIONAL CASE AS IT UNFOLDS.

THE FIRST POLICEMEN TO ARRIVE ARE OFFICERS WILL FITZGERALD AND FRANK PERKINS...

JOINED SHORTLY BY THEIR SUPERIOR, LT. JESS HASKINS.

THESE EXPERIENCED MEN ARE VISIBLY SHAKEN BY WHAT THEY SEE.

EVEN AGGIE UNDERWOOD, ACE CRIME REPORTER FOR THE HERALD EXPRESS, ALMOST KEELS OVER BACKWARD UPON ENCOUNTERING THE SCENE.

TWO SEASONED DETECTIVES FROM CENTRAL HOMICIDE ARE ASSIGNED TO LEAD THE INVESTIGATION: HARRY HANSEN AND FINIS BROWN.

HANSEN, THE SENIOR OFFICER OF THE HOMICIDE DIVISION, IS A 20-YEAR VETERAN WHO HAS WRITTEN A POLICE HANDBOOK ON THE COLLECTION OF EVIDENCE AND THE PRESERVATION OF A CRIME SCENE.

BY THE TIME THEY ARRIVE, AT ABOUT NOON, THE AREA IS ASWARM WITH OFFICERS OF THE UNIVERSITY DIVISION, AS WELL AS MEMBERS OF THE PRESS, LOCAL RESIDENTS, AND PASSERSBY ATTRACTED BY THE ACTIVITY.

14

THE DETECTIVES NOTE THE DISTINGUISHING CHARACTERISTICS OF THE CRIME.

FIRST OF ALL, IT IS OBVIOUS THAT THE YOUNG LADY WAS KILLED ELSEWHERE AND HER BODY PLACED HERE IN A DELIBERATE ARRANGEMENT...

DEPOSITED IN PLAIN SIGHT WHERE ANYONE CAN COME ACROSS IT.

THEY WONDER, IN FACT, THAT IT WAS NOT FOUND MUCH EARLIER.

LIGATURE MARKS ON THE WRISTS AND ANKLES AND AROUND THE NECK...

INDICATE THAT SHE WAS PROBABLY BOUND AND TORTURED PRIOR TO DEATH.

HER MOUTH HAS BEEN SLASHED FROM EAR TO EAR, CREATING A HORRIBLE GRIN.

THE MURDERER TOOK HIS TIME: THIS WAS A MONSTER WHO KNEW WHAT HE WAS DOING.

15

AT LAST, SOMEONE THINKS TO COVER THE REMAINS...
PAGES FROM THE EXAMINER ARE PUT TO USE!

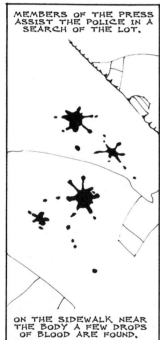

MEMBERS OF THE PRESS ASSIST THE POLICE IN A SEARCH OF THE LOT.

ON THE SIDEWALK NEAR THE BODY A FEW DROPS OF BLOOD ARE FOUND.

A FAINT HEELPRINT, MADE IN THE SAME BLOOD, CAN BE DISCERNED IN THE NEARBY DRIVEWAY.

ALSO A MUDDY TIRE-TRACK.

REMARKABLY, NONE OF THESE CLUES IS PHOTOGRAPHED.

CLOSE TO THE VICTIM IS AN EMPTY CEMENT SACK WITH DROPS OF WATERY BLOOD.

PORTLAND CEMENT

THE DETECTIVES SURMISE THAT IT WAS USED TO CARRY THE TWO HALVES OF THE BODY.

RAY PINKER, HEAD OF THE CRIME LAB, ARRIVES.

THE CONDITION OF THE BODY, HE STATES, IS SO DETERIORATED THAT TIME OF DEATH IS DIFFICULT TO DETERMINE.

HIS BEST ESTIMATE IS THAT SHE HAS BEEN DEAD NO LESS THAN TEN HOURS, AND CERTAINLY NO MORE THAN 24.

THE COLLECTION OF MOISTURE UNDER THE CORPSE INDICATES THAT IT WAS PLACED IN THE LOT BEFORE DAWN.

AT ABOUT 2:45, AN AMBULANCE REMOVES THE BODY TO THE COUNTY MORGUE IN THE BASEMENT OF THE HALL OF JUSTICE DOWNTOWN.

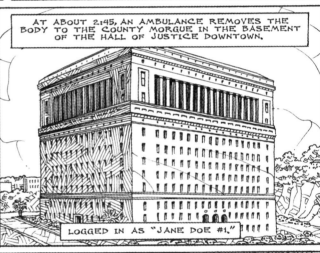

LOGGED IN AS "JANE DOE #1."

HERE, THE HALVES ARE ARRANGED ON A TABLE AND PHOTOGRAPHED FROM EVERY ANGLE.

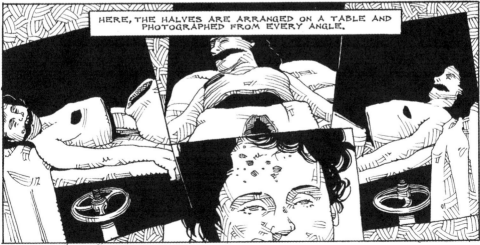

17

**THURSDAY, JANUARY 16**
NEWS OF THE GRISLY CRIME
SENDS THE CITY INTO SHOCK.

THE EXAMINER RUNS AN ARTIST'S
RENDERING OF WHAT THE
RAVAGED VICTIM MIGHT HAVE
LOOKED LIKE.

AT 10:40AM THE POST-MORTEM IS PERFORMED
BY DR. FREDERICK NEWBARR, THE COUNTY'S
CHIEF AUTOPSY SURGEON...

ASSISTED BY DEPUTY CORONER
VICTOR CEFALU

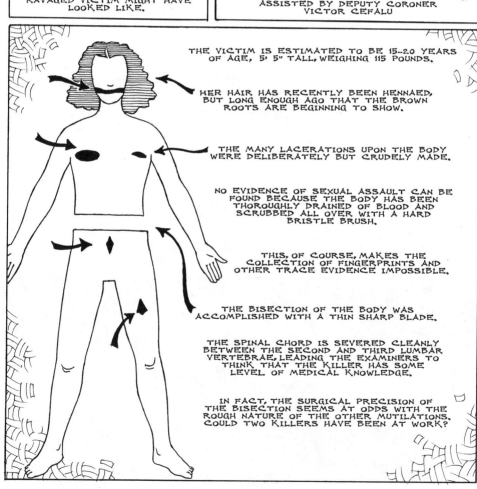

THE VICTIM IS ESTIMATED TO BE 15-20 YEARS
OF AGE, 5' 5" TALL, WEIGHING 115 POUNDS.

HER HAIR HAS RECENTLY BEEN HENNAED,
BUT LONG ENOUGH AGO THAT THE BROWN
ROOTS ARE BEGINNING TO SHOW.

THE MANY LACERATIONS UPON THE BODY
WERE DELIBERATELY BUT CRUDELY MADE.

NO EVIDENCE OF SEXUAL ASSAULT CAN BE
FOUND BECAUSE THE BODY HAS BEEN
THOROUGHLY DRAINED OF BLOOD AND
SCRUBBED ALL OVER WITH A HARD
BRISTLE BRUSH.

THIS, OF COURSE, MAKES THE
COLLECTION OF FINGERPRINTS AND
OTHER TRACE EVIDENCE IMPOSSIBLE.

THE BISECTION OF THE BODY WAS
ACCOMPLISHED WITH A THIN SHARP BLADE.

THE SPINAL CHORD IS SEVERED CLEANLY
BETWEEN THE SECOND AND THIRD LUMBAR
VERTEBRAE, LEADING THE EXAMINERS TO
THINK THAT THE KILLER HAS SOME
LEVEL OF MEDICAL KNOWLEDGE.

IN FACT, THE SURGICAL PRECISION OF
THE BISECTION SEEMS AT ODDS WITH THE
ROUGH NATURE OF THE OTHER MUTILATIONS.
COULD TWO KILLERS HAVE BEEN AT WORK?

THE CAUSE OF DEATH APPEARS TO BE TRAUMA FROM SEVERAL BLOWS TO THE HEAD WITH A HEAVY BLUNT INSTRUMENT...

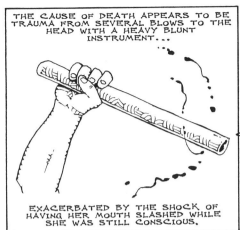

EXACERBATED BY THE SHOCK OF HAVING HER MOUTH SLASHED WHILE SHE WAS STILL CONSCIOUS.

THE MOST EXTREME AND DEGRADING OF THE VIOLATIONS WILL BE KEPT FROM THE PRESS AND PUBLIC...

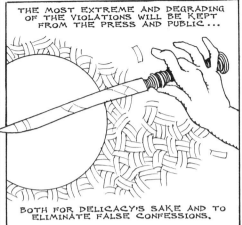

BOTH FOR DELICACY'S SAKE AND TO ELIMINATE FALSE CONFESSIONS.

POLICE AND JOURNALISTS ALIKE ARE CERTAIN THAT, EVEN IN A CITY THAT HAS WITNESSED THE VILEST OF CRIMES...

NO ONE HAS SEEN ANYTHING LIKE THIS.

THE FIRST ORDER OF BUSINESS IS THE IDENTIFICATION OF THE VICTIM.

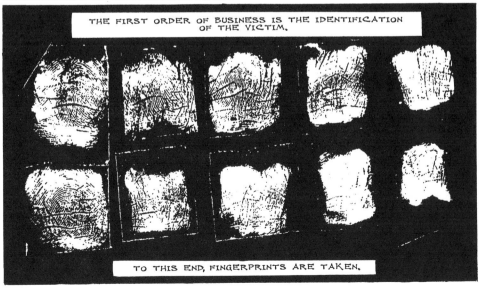

TO THIS END, FINGERPRINTS ARE TAKEN.

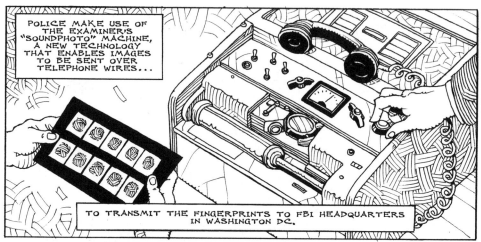

POLICE MAKE USE OF THE EXAMINER'S "SOUNDPHOTO" MACHINE, A NEW TECHNOLOGY THAT ENABLES IMAGES TO BE SENT OVER TELEPHONE WIRES...

TO TRANSMIT THE FINGERPRINTS TO FBI HEADQUARTERS IN WASHINGTON D.C.

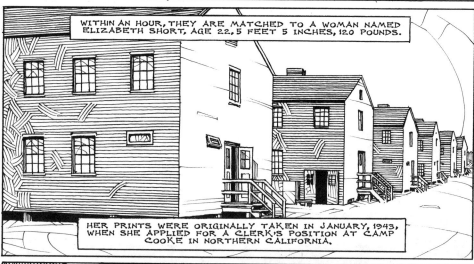

WITHIN AN HOUR, THEY ARE MATCHED TO A WOMAN NAMED ELIZABETH SHORT, AGE 22, 5 FEET 5 INCHES, 120 POUNDS.

HER PRINTS WERE ORIGINALLY TAKEN IN JANUARY, 1943, WHEN SHE APPLIED FOR A CLERK'S POSITION AT CAMP COOKE IN NORTHERN CALIFORNIA.

IT SEEMS SHE ALSO HAD A CRIMINAL RECORD.

IN SEPTEMBER OF THAT YEAR, ANOTHER SET OF PRINTS WAS TAKEN WHEN SHE WAS ARRESTED IN SANTA BARBARA FOR UNDERAGE DRINKING.

A "MUG" SHOT WAS TAKEN AT THE TIME...

AND IT IS NOW DISTRIBUTED TO ALL MEDIA OUTLETS.

IN THIS DAY, WHEN POLICE AND PRESS WORK CLOSELY TOGETHER TO THEIR MUTUAL BENEFIT, BOTH FAN OUT ACROSS THE CITY TO FIND THE POOR YOUNG WOMAN'S FRIENDS AND FAMILY, IF ANY.

BEFORE THE STORY CAN BECOME HEADLINE NEWS NATIONWIDE, HER MOTHER, MRS. PHOEBE SHORT, IS LOCATED IN MEDFORD, MASSACHUSETTS.

ON JANUARY 17, A REPORTER FOR THE EXAMINER, WAYNE SUTTON, IS ORDERED BY HIS EDITOR TO TELEPHONE HER.

IN A QUESTIONABLE PLOY, SUTTON IS DIRECTED TO SAY THAT HE IS PREPARING AN ARTICLE ON HER DAUGHTER, WHO HAS JUST WON A BEAUTY CONTEST...

AND WOULD APPRECIATE ANY INSIGHTS AND INFORMATION SHE MIGHT HAVE.

MRS. SHORT IS OVERJOYED. SHE SAYS THAT ELIZABETH HAS WON SUCH CONTESTS BEFORE IN MASSACHUSETTS.

SHE HAS LATELY BEEN TRYING TO BREAK INTO THE MOVIES AND HAS HAD SOME SMALL PARTS.

THE LAST TIME SHE HEARD FROM HER, SHE WAS LIVING IN SAN DIEGO AND WORKING AT THE NAVAL HOSPITAL THERE.

IT IS NOT LONG BEFORE THE REPORTER BEGINS TO REGRET HIS RUSE.

AT LAST HE BREAKS THE TERRIBLE NEWS, SAYING THAT HE HAD TO MAKE SURE SHE WAS THE RIGHT PERSON.

AS CONSOLATION, THE EXAMINER OFFERS TO PAY HER WAY TO LOS ANGELES FOR THE INQUEST.

# PART TWO

# THE LIFE OF
# ELIZABETH SHORT

TO APPEARANCES, SHE LIVED A TYPICAL
AMERICAN GIRLHOOD...

IN THE SUBURBS OF BOSTON.

SHE WAS BORN JULY 29, 1924, IN HYDE PARK, MASSACHUSETTS...

THE MIDDLE OF FIVE DAUGHTERS.

VIRGINIA | DOROTHEA | ELIZABETH | ELEANORA | MURIEL

BORN TO PHOEBE AND HER HUSBAND CLEO SHORT.

THE FATHER WAS ABLE TO PROVIDE A COMFORTABLE LIVING FOR HIS FAMILY BY CATCHING THE LATEST CRAZE: MINIATURE GOLF.

HE BUILT AND OPERATED SEVERAL COURSES IN THE BOSTON AREA.

IN 1926, HE MOVED THEM TO A LARGE HOME IN NEARBY MEDFORD.

MEDFORD

BOSTON

HYDE PARK

THESE WERE HAPPY YEARS.

THE STOCK MARKET
CRASH OF 1929 PLUNGED
CLEO SHORT INTO
BANKRUPTCY.

IN 1930, HE STAGED A SUICIDE BY ABANDONING
HIS CAR ON THE CHARLES RIVER BRIDGE...

AND VANISHING FROM THE CITY.

THE FAMILY HE LEFT BEHIND WAS NOW
ON THE BRINK OF DESTITUTION.

PHEOBE MADE A LIVING AS BEST
SHE COULD...

MOVING OFTEN, AS NEW AND CHEAPER
HOUSING COULD BE FOUND.

WHENEVER MONEY COULD BE
SCRAPED TOGETHER FOR
AMUSEMENT, "BETTY" AND
HER SISTERS WOULD ATTEND
THE MOVIES.

ENCHANTED BY THE IMAGES ONSCREEN,
SHE DREAMED OF BEING A STAR.

25

AS SHE GREW, BETTY WAS PLAGUED BY ASTHMA AND OTHER RESPIRATORY PROBLEMS...

AT AGE 16, DURING HER SOPHOMORE YEAR, SHE DROPPED OUT OF HIGH SCHOOL AND BEGAN SPENDING WINTERS IN MIAMI BEACH, FLORIDA.

ENDURING, AT ONE POINT, SERIOUS LUNG SURGERY.

SHE LIVED AT FIRST WITH FAMILY FRIENDS...

AND MADE A SMALL INCOME WAITING TABLES.

UPON HER RETURN TO MEDFORD, THOSE WHO KNEW HER NOTICED A NEWLY-ACQUIRED GLAMOUR AND SOPHISTICATION.

SHE TURNED HEADS WHEREVER SHE WENT.

LATE IN 1942, A LETTER ARRIVED FROM CLEO SHORT, VERY MUCH ALIVE, IN NORTHERN CALIFORNIA.

HE DESIRED, IT SEEMED, TO RECONNECT WITH HIS ABANDONED FAMILY.

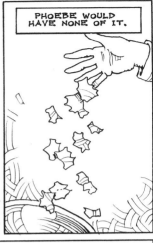

PHOEBE WOULD HAVE NONE OF IT.

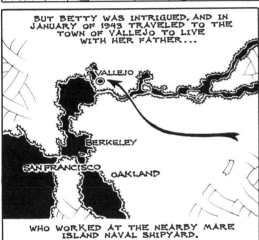

BUT BETTY WAS INTRIGUED, AND IN JANUARY OF 1943 TRAVELED TO THE TOWN OF VALLEJO TO LIVE WITH HER FATHER...

VALLEJO

BERKELEY

SAN FRANCISCO    OAKLAND

WHO WORKED AT THE NEARBY MARE ISLAND NAVAL SHIPYARD.

SHE STILL HARBORED AMBITIONS TO BREAK INTO THE MOVIES, AND THIS WAS A LITTLE CLOSER TO HOLLYWOOD.

IN PRACTICALLY NO TIME, HOWEVER, SERIOUS RIFTS DEVELOPED BETWEEN FATHER AND DAUGHTER.

HE WAS DISGUSTED WITH HER MESSY HABITS, HER REVEALING OUTFITS, HER NIGHTLY DATES WITH SAILORS.

SHE COMPLAINED THAT ALL HE WANTED WAS A COOK AND HOUSEKEEPER.

SO IT WAS NOT LONG BEFORE SHE CAUGHT A RIDE WITH A SOLDIER...

SAN FRANCISCO
SAN JOSE
MONTEREY
LOMPOC
SANTA BARBARA

AND MOVED SOUTH TO CAMP COOKE, NEAR LOMPOC.

NOW CALLING HERSELF BETH, SHE FOUND WORK AS A CASHIER AT THE POST EXCHANGE...

AND IMMEDIATELY BECAME A MAGNET FOR THE LONELY YOUNG MEN STATIONED THERE.

THEY VOTED HER "CAMP CUTIE."

EVERYONE TOLD HER THAT SHE COULD BE A MOVIE STAR.

EARLY ON, SHE ACQUIRED A REPUTATION OF "LOOK BUT DON'T TOUCH."

SHE WOULD PROVIDE A PLEASANT EVENING'S COMPANIONSHIP BUT NEVER GO "ALL THE WAY."

IN TIME, BETH LEFT HER JOB AND LIVED IN A HOUSE WITH OTHER YOUNG WOMEN IN SANTA BARBARA.

IN SEPTEMBER OF 1943, SHE WAS OUT ON THE TOWN WITH A LOUD PARTY OF SOLDIERS AND GIRLS...

WHEN POLICE WERE SUMMONED.

ALTHOUGH SHE HAD NOT BEEN DRINKING, SHE WAS PART OF A GROUP THAT HAD...

AND SINCE SHE WAS ONLY 19, BETH WAS CHARGED WITH VIOLATING CALIFORNIA'S LIQUOR LAW.

SHE WAS RELEASED ON PROBATION, BUT HER FED-UP FATHER REFUSED TO ACCEPT CUSTODY...

AND SO SHE WAS PUT ON A BUS AND SHIPPED HOME TO MEDFORD.

THERE, SHE WORKED SPORADICALLY AS A WAITRESS AND MOVIE THEATRE USHERETTE.

BUT LIFE AT HOME ONCE AGAIN PROVED TOO CONFINING FOR HER RESTLESS SPIRIT...

AND THE WINTER OF 1943-44 FOUND HER BACK IN MIAMI.

IT WAS NOT LONG BEFORE SHE WAS NOTICED BY A MODELING AGENT NAMED DUFFY SAWYER...

AND, THROUGH HIS CONTACTS, OBTAINED ASSIGNMENTS THAT TOOK HER TO CHICAGO AND INDIANAPOLIS...

MODELING HATS, GLOVES, AND JEWELRY.

BUT THIS WORK WAS ANYTHING BUT STEADY.

BY NIGHT, SHE MADE THE ROUNDS OF BARS AND NIGHTCLUBS, ALWAYS ON THE ARM OF A SOLDIER OR SAILOR.

AT LAST, SOMETIME IN MID 1944, SHE ARRIVED IN LOS ANGELES THE CITY OF HER DREAMS.

SHE FOUND VARIOUS LIVING ARRANGEMENTS WITH OTHER YOUNG LADIES LIKE HERSELF: FRINGE DWELLERS AMBITIOUS TO BECOME STARS OR IN SOME WAY ENTER THE GLAMOROUS LIFE OF THE PICTURE CAPITAL...

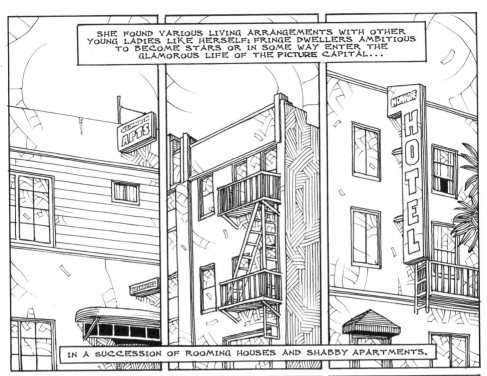

IN A SUCCESSION OF ROOMING HOUSES AND SHABBY APARTMENTS.

FOR A TIME, SHE SHARED A ROOM WITH ANOTHER ASPIRING ACTRESS, LUCILLE VERELLA...

AT THE CLINTON HOTEL IN DOWNTOWN LOS ANGELES.

TOGETHER, THEY MADE THE ROUNDS OF CASTING OFFICES AND MODELING AGENCIES.

WITH NO ASSIGNMENTS FORTHCOMING, BETH ONCE AGAIN FOUND HERSELF WAITING TABLES.

31

MOST IMPORTANT WAS TO BE "SEEN."

TO THIS END, SHE AND LUCILLE WOULD STROLL ALONG HOLLYWOOD BOULEVARD, BROWSING THE STORE WINDOWS, FLIRTING WITH SOLDIERS.

Special
MARKED DOWN

THEY HUNG OUT AT THE FOUR-STAR GRILLE ON MELROSE AVENUE, WHERE THEY COULD MINGLE WITH SHOW BUSINESS PEOPLE.

ST·LUNCH·DINN

CHOPS STEAKS

IT WAS DURING THIS TIME THAT BETH DEVELOPED HER DISTINCTIVE AND WELL-REMEMBERED LOOK: ALL BLACK OUTFITS, JET BLACK HAIR, PALE COMPLEXION, WITH BRILLIANT RED LIPS AND NAILS.

SHE ATTRACTED THE EYE OF EVERYONE SHE PASSED.

*hollywood Canteen*

IN THE EVENINGS, SHE VOLUNTEERED AT THE HOLLYWOOD CANTEEN, THAT WARTIME INSTITUTION WHERE LONELY SERVICEMEN COULD RUB ELBOWS WITH MOVIE ROYALTY.

THERE, SHE COULD DANCE WITH AS MANY SOLDIERS AS SHE LIKED AND, INCIDENTALLY, RECEIVE FREE MEALS.

MEN NATURALLY FLOCKED TO HER.

AND IT WAS HERE THAT BETH FOUND HER FIRST SERIOUS BOYFRIEND: LT. GORDON FICKLING OF THE ARMY AIR CORPS.

HE WAS DASHING AND MAGNETIC, AND THEY SEEMED A PERFECT MATCH.

BUT HE SHIED AWAY FROM A PERMANENT COMMITMENT, SINCE HE WAS ABOUT TO BE SENT OVERSEAS.

THEY WILL REMAIN IN TOUCH OVER THE YEARS TO COME.

THE CANTEEN REMAINED HOLLYWOOD'S MOST FAMOUS VENUE FOR ROMANCE, HEARTBREAK...AND TRAGEDY.

IN OCTOBER, 1944, THE 20-YEAR-OLD HEIRESS GEORGETTE BAUERDORFF, A JUNIOR HOSTESS THERE, WAS MURDERED...

STRANGLED TO DEATH, RAPED AND BEATEN, HER NUDE BODY LEFT IN THE BATHTUB OF HER WEST HOLLYWOOD APARTMENT.

THE PERPETRATOR WAS NEVER FOUND.

THAT WINTER, BETH RETURNED TO MIAMI.

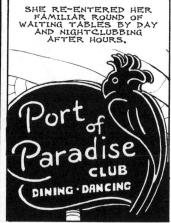

SHE RE-ENTERED HER FAMILIAR ROUND OF WAITING TABLES BY DAY AND NIGHTCLUBBING AFTER HOURS.

34

ON THE LAST DAY OF 1944, SHE MET AND FELL IN LOVE WITH MATT GORDON, A HANDSOME CAPTAIN WITH THE FAMED FLYING TIGERS...

RECIPIENT OF THE DISTINGUISHED FLYING CROSS, THE SILVER AND BRONZE STARS, A HERO IN EVERY WAY.

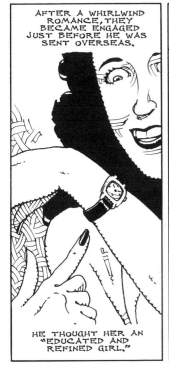

AFTER A WHIRLWIND ROMANCE, THEY BECAME ENGAGED JUST BEFORE HE WAS SENT OVERSEAS.

HE THOUGHT HER AN "EDUCATED AND REFINED GIRL."

IN APRIL, 1945, BETH RETURNED TO HER MOTHER'S HOME IN MEDFORD...

TO PREPARE FOR THE WEDDING, WHICH WAS PLANNED FOR THE COMING SUMMER.

SHE CONFIDED TO A FRIEND THAT SHE WAS STILL A VIRGIN.

ON MAY 8, 1945, THE WAR IN EUROPE ENDED...

TO GENERAL EXTASY, AS THOUSANDS OF SERVICE-MEN CAME HOME.

BUT BETH'S HAPPINESS WAS NOT TO LAST: IN AUGUST, SHE RECEIVED A TELEGRAM FROM MATT'S MOTHER, ALONG WITH A NEWSPAPER CLIPPING.

ON HIS WAY BACK FROM THE PACIFIC THEATRE, HIS PLANE WAS SHOT DOWN OVER INDIA.

PLUNGED INTO DESPAIR, HER LIFE DEVOLVED INTO ITS FORMER AIMLESS PATTERN.

SHE RETURNED TO MIAMI FOR THE WINTER OF 1945-46, AND THEN BRIEFLY BACK TO MEDFORD.

IN APRIL, SHE TRAVELED TO CHICAGO, AGAIN UNDER THE AUSPICES OF DUFFY SAWYER.

WHEN NO MODELING JOBS TURNED UP, SHE SERVED AS A HOSTESS FOR THE AGENT, ADORNING THE TABLE WHEN HE ENTERTAINED PROSPECTIVE CLIENTS.

IT WAS ALSO IN CHICAGO THAT SHE RECONNECTED WITH LT. GORDON FICKLING, AND THEIR ROMANCE REKINDLED.

# PART THREE

# HER LAST DAYS

IN JULY OF 1946, BETH SHORT RETURNED TO SOUTHERN CALIFORNIA FOR A FINAL TIME.

AS NEARLY AS CAN BE RECONSTRUCTED, THESE WERE HER LAST DAYS.

SHE SET UP RESIDENCE IN THE WATER HOTEL IN LONG BEACH...

TO BE NEAR FICKLING, WHO WAS STATIONED AT THE NEARBY ARMY AIR BASE.

BUT THEIR LOVE AFFAIR SOON COOLED.

HE WAS JEALOUS OF HER FLIRTATIOUSNESS; SHE FELT LIKE A KEPT WOMAN.

SHE OFTEN STOPPED AT THE SODA FOUNTAIN OF A LOCAL DRUG STORE...

WHERE SHE COULD COUNT ON ATTRACTING MASCULINE ATTENTION.

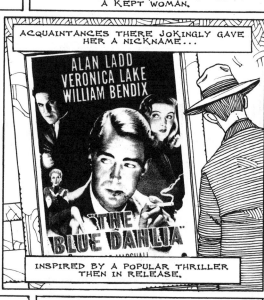

ACQUAINTANCES THERE JOKINGLY GAVE HER A NICKNAME...

INSPIRED BY A POPULAR THRILLER THEN IN RELEASE.

BETH SHORT WOULD FOREVER BE REMEMBERED AS...

THE BLACK DAHLIA!

WITH MARRIAGE NOT IN THE CARDS, FICKLING, DISCHARGED FROM THE SERVICE, MOVED TO NORTH CAROLINA.

THEY WILL CONTINUE TO EXCHANGE LETTERS.

BETH MOVED TO HOLLYWOOD, TO LIVE ONCE AGAIN IN A SERIES OF CHEAP HOTELS AND CRAMPED APARTMENTS.

FOR A TIME, SHE ROOMED WITH MARJORIE GRAHAM, AN OLD ACQUAINTANCE FROM MASSACHUSETTS...

HAWTHORNE HOTEL

CHANCELLOR HOTEL

TAMARIND APARTMENTS

AND LYNN MARTIN, A 16-YEAR-OLD ASPIRING ACTRESS, WHO COULD PASS FOR A WOMAN MUCH OLDER.

EVEN SO, SHE HAD FEW REAL FRIENDS OR CONFIDANTS.

OTHER WOMEN FOUND HER MYSTERIOUS AND SECRETIVE

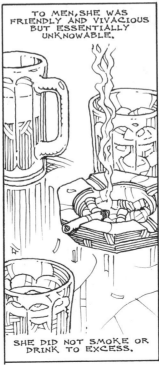

TO MEN, SHE WAS FRIENDLY AND VIVACIOUS BUT ESSENTIALLY UNKNOWABLE.

SHE DID NOT SMOKE OR DRINK TO EXCESS.

NOR WAS SHE SEXUALLY ADVENTUROUS.

NEVERTHELESS, SHE KNEW HOW TO GET WHAT SHE WANTED FROM A MAN.

TYPICAL OF HER ENCOUNTERS AT THIS TIME WAS THE MANAGER OF A CERTAIN SHOE STORE ON HOLLYWOOD BOULEVARD.

THOUGH MARRIED, HE KEPT AN EYE OUT FOR THE LADIES.

ONE DAY, HE NOTICED BETH AS SHE BROWSED THE NEW SHOES.

SHE HAD NO MONEY, BUT HE SET ASIDE A PAIR SHE WANTED.

TWO DAYS LATER, HE TOOK HER TO LUNCH, AND ENDED UP LENDING HER MONEY AND GIVING HER THE SHOES.

FROM THEN ON, SHE DROPPED INTO THE STORE PERIODICALLY.

HE WOULD GIVE HER A LITTLE CASH AND DRIVE HER HOME IN HIS CAR.

THEY ENGAGED IN SESSIONS OF HEAVY PETTING, BUT SHE DREW THE LINE AT ANYTHING FURTHER.

NEVERTHELESS, HE CONTINUED TO GIVE HER NEW SHOES AND, ONCE, A PURSE.

THE LAST TIME HE SAW HER SHE CAME INTO THE STORE ON THE ARM OF A SHORT "GREASY-LOOKING" MAN, OBVIOUSLY A NEW BOYFRIEND.

BY THIS TIME, BETH HAD BECOME PART OF THE CROWD SURROUNDING THE NIGHTCLUB OWNER MARK HANSEN.

HANSEN WAS PROPRIETOR OF THE FLORENTINE GARDENS ON HOLLYWOOD BOULEVARD...

WHOSE "FLESH AND FANTASY" REVUE BROUGHT IN EAGER CROWDS NIGHTLY.

HE LIVED IN A MANSION ON CARLOS STREET BEHIND THE CLUB.

HE ALSO OWNED APARTMENTS AND ROOMING HOUSES AROUND TOWN...

IN WHICH HE RENTED SPACE TO SHOWGIRLS AT THE CLUB, AS WELL AS TO OTHER YOUNG WOMEN TRYING TO MAKE IT IN HOLLYWOOD.

FOR A TIME, BETH ROOMED AT HANSEN'S HOUSE WITH THE ACTRESS ANN TOTH...

WHO HAPPENED TO BE THE OWNER'S GIRLFRIEND.

THOUGH NEVER AN ACTUAL EMPLOYEE, BETH BECAME A "REGULAR" AT THE CLUB.

HER MAGNETIC PERSONALITY GUARANTEED THE ATTENTION OF THE WELL-HEELED MALE CUSTOMERS.

AT THE FLORENTINE GARDENS, SHE FOUND AMPLE
OPPORTUNITY TO SEARCH OUT AN IDEAL MATE...

EVEN IF HE MIGHT BE OF A DOUBTFUL KIND.

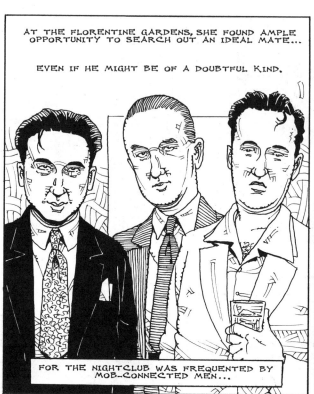

FOR THE NIGHTCLUB WAS FREQUENTED BY
MOB-CONNECTED MEN...

CHIEF AMONG THEM
BENJAMIN "BUGSY"
SIEGEL ...

ONE OF THE FOUNDING
FATHERS OF WEST COAST
ORGANIZED CRIME.

AT THIS TIME,
THE GANGS OPERATE
UNIMPEDED ON THE
STREETS OF LOS
ANGELES...

DUE TO STRATEGIC
PAYOFFS AT CERTAIN
LEVELS OF THE LAPD.

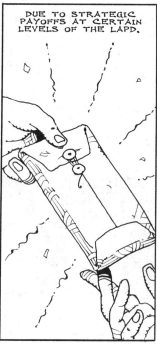

THE DEPARTMENT'S
GANGSTER SQUAD WAS
MORE CONCERNED WITH
FACILITATING CRIMINAL
ACTIVITIES THAN IN
OBSTRUCTING THEM.

LATE IN 1946, BETH LIVED AT THE CHANCELLOR HOTEL ON CHEROKEE AVENUE...

IN A TWO-BEDROOM APARTMENT WITH SEVEN OTHER WOMEN!

HER ROOM-MATES WILL LATER RECALL THAT SHE WAS EVER IN NEED, BORROWING MONEY, CLOTHING, COSMETICS.

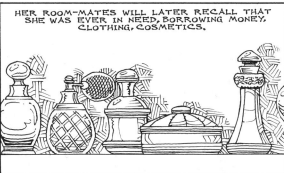

WITH NO FUNDS TO SEE A DENTIST, HER TEETH WERE IN AN ADVANCED STATE OF DECAY.

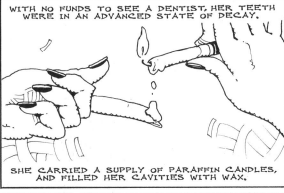

SHE CARRIED A SUPPLY OF PARAFFIN CANDLES, AND FILLED HER CAVITIES WITH WAX.

HER OLD DREAM OF MOVIE STARDOM HAD APPARENTLY FALLEN BY THE WAYSIDE.

IT NOW SEEMED THAT ALL SHE WANTED WAS TO MARRY AND SETTLE INTO DOMESTICITY.

KEEPING UP HER APPEARANCE BECAME EVER MORE ESSENTIAL.

SHE FUSSED FOR HOURS BEFORE THE MIRROR.

AT THIS TIME, SHE WAS OFTEN SEEN IN THE COMPANY OF A MINOR MOBSTER NAMED MAURICE CLEMENT...

A MINION OF "BUGSY" SIEGEL AND HIS COHORT, MICKEY COHEN.

CLEMENT WAS A PROCUROR FOR THE MOB'S PROSTITUTION RING AND CHAUFFEURED THE LADIES TO THEIR VARIOUS APPOINTMENTS.

HE CALLED FOR BETH AT WHATEVER RESIDENCE SHE HAPPENED TO BE... BUT WAS HE MERELY A GO-BETWEEN?

WITH WHAT KIND OF SHADY CHARACTERS WAS SHE BECOMING INVOLVED?

HER INNOCENT, UNWORLDLY DEMEANOR WAS NOT AN ACT. SHE WOULD HAVE BEEN AN EASY MARK FOR ANY PREDATOR.

TOWARD THE END OF 1946, HER ROOM-MATES NOTICED THAT SHE SEEMED WORRIED AND DISTRACTED, AS IF IN FEAR OF SOMETHING UNKNOWN.

SHE HENNAED HER HAIR TO A DARK RED.

FRIDAY, DECEMBER 6
SHE TOLD PEOPLE THAT SHE WAS GOING UP TO BERKELEY TO VISIT HER SISTER...

BUT INSTEAD, ON BORROWED MONEY, SHE BOARDED A GREYHOUND BUS AND WENT SOUTH TO SAN DIEGO.

BETH'S FIRST NIGHT THERE FOUND HER ASLEEP IN WHAT SHE THOUGHT WAS AN ALL-NIGHT MOVIE THEATRE.

BUT IT CLOSED AT MIDNIGHT, AND SHE WAS AWAKENED BY THE CASHIER, DOROTHY FRENCH.

THE 21-YEAR-OLD TOOK PITY ON THE LOST YOUNG WOMAN, WHO HAD A BAD COUGH AND DID NOT LOOK ANY TOO HEALTHY.

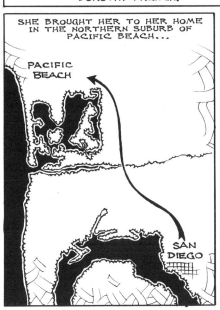

SHE BROUGHT HER TO HER HOME IN THE NORTHERN SUBURB OF PACIFIC BEACH...

PACIFIC BEACH

SAN DIEGO

WHERE SHE LIVED WITH HER MOTHER, ELVERA, AND YOUNGER BROTHER, CORY.

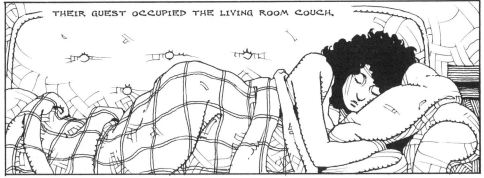

THEIR GUEST OCCUPIED THE LIVING ROOM COUCH.

45

BETH ASSURED THE FAMILY THAT SHE WAS APPLYING FOR A JOB AT THE NAVAL HOSPITAL...

AND WOULD BE TROUBLING THEM FOR NO MORE THAN A DAY OR TWO.

SHE TOLD THEM THAT HER HUSBAND HAD BEEN KILLED IN THE WAR, AND BROUGHT OUT MATT GORDON'S OBITUARY.

DECORATED OFFICER DEAD IN AIR CRASH

SHE HAD CROSSED OUT THE WORD "FIANCEE," CLAIMING IT WAS A MISPRINT, AND WRITTEN IN "WIFE."

BUT THE DAYS STRETCHED INTO WEEKS.

SHE LOUNGED INTO THE AFTERNOON IN A SILK CHINESE ROBE...

HER CLOTHES STREWN ABOUT THE LIVING ROOM, HER HEAVY PERFUME FILLING THE HOUSE.

SHE SPENT DAYS WRITING LETTERS TO WHAT SHE CALLED HER "HOLLYWOOD CONNECTIONS."

EVEN HERE, BETH SHORT HAD NO TROUBLE FINDING DATES.

ONE SUCH YOUNG MAN WAS ROBERT "RED" MANLEY, A 25-YEAR-OLD TRAVELING SALESMAN.

THEY MET ON A DOWNTOWN STREET CORNER.

ALTHOUGH MARRIED, WITH A YOUNG SON, HE WAS INSTANTLY ATTRACTED TO HER.

TO MANLEY, SHE SEEMED AT TIMES TO BE AFRAID OF SOMETHING.

SHE TOLD HIM THAT SHE WAS RUNNING AWAY FROM A VIOLENT BOYFRIEND.

TO THE FRENCHES, IT OFTEN LOOKED AS IF SHE WERE HIDING OUT IN THEIR HOME.

ONE EVENING, THREE STRANGERS, TWO MEN AND A WOMAN, KNOCKED AT THE FRONT DOOR.

BETH HID AROUND A CORNER AND BEGGED MRS. FRENCH NOT TO ANSWER.

IN TIME, THE THREE DEPARTED.

AS THE YEAR 1947 DAWNED, BETH'S SITUATION REMAINED UNCHANGED.

MRS. FRENCH HAD BECOME DISGUSTED WITH THEIR GUEST'S MESSY HABITS.

SHE COMPLAINED OF HER STRIDING ABOUT IN HER LOOSE ROBE IN FRONT OF YOUNG CORY.

DOROTHY, HOWEVER, STILL FELT SORRY FOR THE LOST SOUL.

BUT AT LAST, MOTHER AND DAUGHTER ASKED HER TO LEAVE.

BETH, WHO HAD RECENTLY RECEIVED A WINDFALL OF $100 FROM GORDON FICKLING, AGREED READILY ENOUGH.

WEDNESDAY, JANUARY 8, 1947
THAT AFTERNOON, SHE WAS CALLED FOR BY "RED" MANLEY, AND THE TWO DROVE NORTH.

THEY SPENT A CHASTE NIGHT AT A MOTEL.

THERE, HE NOTICED SEVERAL SERIOUS SCRATCHES ON HER ARM...

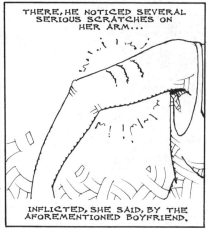

INFLICTED, SHE SAID, BY THE AFOREMENTIONED BOYFRIEND.

48

THE NEXT DAY, THEY CONTINUED NORTHWARD.

BETH SEEMED NERVOUS, PEERING INTO THE OTHER CARS THEY PASSED ON THE HIGHWAY.

AT A REST STOP, SHE MADE A TELEPHONE CALL...

AFTER WHICH SHE INFORMED MANLEY THAT SHE WOULD MEET HER SISTER IN LOS ANGELES, TRAVEL WITH HER TO BERKELEY, AND THEN MOVE BACK HOME TO BOSTON.

THEY ARRIVED IN DOWNTOWN LOS ANGELES ON THE AFTERNOON OF JANUARY 9.

BETH CHECKED HER BAGS AT THE GREYHOUND BUS DEPOT.

AT 6:30PM, MANLEY TOOK HER TO THE BILTMORE HOTEL, THERE, PRESUMABLY, TO MEET HER SISTER.

HE SAT WITH HER IN THE LOBBY FOR A WHILE...

AND THEN RELUCTANTLY DEPARTED.

FOR THE REST OF THE EVENING, SHE WAS SEEN BY HOTEL EMPLOYEES MAKING PHONE CALLS, WATCHING THE DOOR EXPECTANTLY.

AT 10PM, SHE FINALLY LEFT THE HOTEL. THE DOORMAN WATCHED HER WALK SOUTH ON OLIVE STREET.

IT WAS THE LAST VERIFIED TIME THAT ANYBODY SAW HER ALIVE.

# PART IV

# THE INVESTIGATION

UNDER THE OVERALL SUPERVISION OF
CAPT. JACK DONAHOE OF CENTRAL HOMICIDE...

THE INVESTIGATION WILL EVENTUALLY EMPLOY THE
ENERGIES OF 700 OFFICERS FROM THE LAPD, AS WELL AS
400 COUNTY SHERIFF'S DEPUTIES, 250 HIGHWAY PATROL
OFFICERS, AND DOZENS OF LOCAL PRIVATE DETECTIVES.

FORTY OFFICERS COMB THE VACANT LOT.

A MILITARY-STYLE WRISTWATCH IS FOUND NEAR WHERE THE BODY LAY, BUT NOTHING WILL BE LEARNED FROM IT.

VICE DETECTIVES GO DOOR-TO-DOOR, INTERVIEWING RESIDENTS ON THE SURROUNDING STREETS.

IN THE FIRST HOURS MORE THAN 150 KNOWN SEX OFFENDERS ARE SCREENED AND CLEARED.

TRASH BINS AND SEWERS IN THE AREA ARE GIVEN PARTICULAR SCRUTINY.

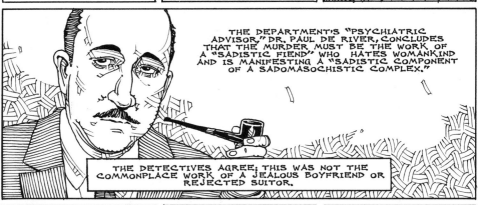

THE DEPARTMENT'S "PSYCHIATRIC ADVISOR," DR. PAUL DE RIVER, CONCLUDES THAT THE MURDER MUST BE THE WORK OF A "SADISTIC FIEND" WHO HATES WOMANKIND AND IS MANIFESTING A "SADISTIC COMPONENT OF A SADOMASOCHISTIC COMPLEX."

THE DETECTIVES AGREE: THIS WAS NOT THE COMMONPLACE WORK OF A JEALOUS BOYFRIEND OR REJECTED SUITOR.

THE MURDERER WOULD HAVE NEEDED A HOUSE, WITH THE TIME AND PRIVACY TO COMPLETE THE DEED...

NOT TO MENTION HIS OWN CAR TO TRANSPORT THE REMAINS.

MANY ARE PUT IN MIND OF CLEVELAND'S INFAMOUS "TORSO" MURDERS OF A DECADE AGO.

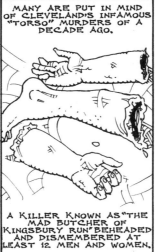

A KILLER KNOWN AS "THE MAD BUTCHER OF KINGSBURY RUN" BEHEADED AND DISMEMBERED AT LEAST 12 MEN AND WOMEN.

IN SOME INSTANCES, THE TORSO WAS CUT IN HALF.

THE PERPETRATOR WAS NEVER APPREHENDED.

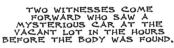

TWO WITNESSES COME FORWARD WHO SAW A MYSTERIOUS CAR AT THE VACANT LOT IN THE HOURS BEFORE THE BODY WAS FOUND.

BOBBY JONES, A NEWSPAPER CARRIER, AND ROBERT MEYER, A LOCAL RESIDENT, SAW AN OLDER MODEL BLACK SEDAN STOP AT THE CURB AND WAIT THERE 4-5 MINUTES.

THIS WAS AT ABOUT 6AM. NEITHER GOT A GOOD LOOK AT THE DRIVER.

WHERE WAS ELIZABETH SHORT FROM JANUARY 9TH TO THE 15TH?

AN EFFORT IS MADE TO FILL IN THE FINAL WEEK OF HER LIFE.

A POLICEWOMAN, MYRL McBRIDE, IDENTIFIES SHORT AS THE WOMAN SHE SAW AT A DOWNTOWN BUS STATION ON JANUARY 14, "SOBBING IN TERROR" AND AFRAID TO GO BACK INTO A BAR TO RETRIEVE HER PURSE.

LATER, McBRIDE WILL BACK DOWN, UNCERTAIN AS TO WHETHER IT WAS THE RIGHT WOMAN.

MR. AND MRS. WILLIAM JOHNSON, WHO RUN A MOTEL ON EAST WASHINGTON BLVD., CLAIM TO HAVE SEEN SHORT ON JANUARY 12, WHEN SHE AND A MAN CHECKED IN AS HUSBAND AND WIFE.

BUT POLICE ARE DOUBTFUL OF THEIR IDENTIFICATION, SINCE THEY SAY THE GIRL HAD JET-BLACK HAIR, WHILE IT IS KNOWN THAT SHORT HAD COLORED HERS A DARK RED.

WITH NO RELIABLE WITNESSES AS TO THE MISSING DAYS...

POLICE NOW SPECULATE THAT SHE MIGHT HAVE BEEN HELD CAPTIVE FOR THAT ENTIRE WEEK.

MORE THAN 20 OF THE VICTIM'S BOYFRIENDS AND ESCORTS ARE SOUGHT OUT AND INTERVIEWED.

ALL ARE ELIMINATED AS SUSPECTS.

BETH SHORT'S MOTHER DIRECTS INVESTIGATORS TO THE FRENCHES IN SAN DIEGO...

WHO, IN TURN, POINT THEM TO THE YOUNG MAN WHO CALLED FOR THEIR GUEST.

"RED" MANLEY IS FOUND AT HIS HOME IN HUNTINGTON PARK...

AND BROUGHT IN FOR QUESTIONING.

FOR A WHILE, MANLEY IS THE CHIEF SUSPECT.

AT POLICE HEADQUARTERS DOWNTOWN HE IS GIVEN AN INTENSE "GRILLING."

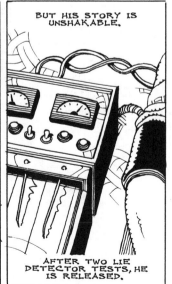

BUT HIS STORY IS UNSHAKABLE.

AFTER TWO LIE DETECTOR TESTS, HE IS RELEASED.

THE SUITCASES LEFT BY ELIZABETH SHORT AT THE DOWNTOWN GREYHOUND STATION ARE RECOVERED BY POLICE.

THEIR CONTENTS WILL NEVER BE RELEASED TO THE PUBLIC.

HOWEVER, A PAIR OF BAGS THAT SHE LEFT AT THE BUS DEPOT IN SAN DIEGO ARE RETRIEVED BY REPORTERS FOR THE EXAMINER...

AS IS A TRUNK, LOST IN TRANSIT FROM CHICAGO, FOUND AT THE RAILWAY EXPRESS OFFICE IN LOS ANGELES.

INSIDE, AMONG THE CLOTHING AND COSMETICS, ARE FOUND SEVERAL ALBUMS AND SCRAPBOOKS CONTAINING DOZENS OF PHOTOS FROM HAPPIER TIMES.

MOST OF THEM SHOW HER IN THE COMPANY OF MEN...
MANY ARE SOLDIERS...
SOME ARE OLDER...
SOME YOUNG.

EFFORTS ARE MADE TO LOCATE ALL OF THEM.

AMONG THE SEVERAL PACKETS OF LETTERS AND CARDS IS FOUND THE TELEGRAM FROM MATT GORDON'S MOTHER, INFORMING BETH OF HER FIANCEE'S DEATH.

WESTERN UNION

MANY OF THE LETTERS (APPARENTLY NEVER SENT) ARE PASSIONATE MESSAGES FROM BETH TO MATT GORDON, GORDON FICKLING, AND VARIOUS OTHER MALE FRIENDS.

"I LOVE YOU, I LOVE YOU, I LOVE YOU, SWEETHEART OF ALL MY DREAMS...OH MATT, HONESTLY, I SUPPOSE WHEN TWO PEOPLE ARE IN LOVE AS WE ARE OUR LETTERS SOUND OUT OF THIS WORLD TO A CENSOR..."

OTHERS ARE TO HER FROM SOME OF THE SAME MEN, TRYING TO COOL THEIR RELATIONSHIP.

USO

"WHEN YOU MENTIONED MARRIAGE IN YOUR LETTER, BETH, I GOT TO WONDERING ABOUT MYSELF. SEEMS LIKE YOU HAVE TO BE IN LOVE WITH A PERSON BEFORE IT'S A SAFE BET. INFATUATION IS SOMETIMES MISTAKENLY ACCEPTED FOR TRUE LOVE, WHICH CAN NEVER BE."

"TIME AND AGAIN I'VE SUGGESTED THAT YOU FORGET ME, AS I'VE BELIEVED IT'S THE ONLY THING FOR YOU TO DO TO BE HAPPY."

56

WEDNESDAY, JANUARY 22
A POLICE CIRCULAR WITH A PHOTOGRAPH AND DESCRIPTION OF THE VICTIM IS ISSUED...

AND POSTED IN THE CITY'S BUS STATIONS, HOTELS, BARS, AND NIGHTCLUBS.

ON THE SAME DAY, THE CORONER'S INQUEST IS HELD AT THE DOWNTOWN HALL OF JUSTICE.

OFFICE OF THE CORONER

568

CLEO SHORT, NOW LIVING IN THE CITY, IS STILL DISGUSTED WITH HIS WAYWARD DAUGHTER AND HAS REFUSED TO IDENTIFY THE REMAINS.

BETH'S MOTHER, PHOEBE, HAS FLOWN IN FROM MASSACHUSETTS.

SHE AND HER DAUGHTER, VIRGINIA, PERFORM THE GRIM TASK.

THE INQUEST, AT WHICH NO CORONER'S REPORT IS PRESENTED, LASTS 45 MINUTES...

AND CONCLUDES, TO NO ONE'S SURPRISE, WITH A VERDICT OF MURDER BY PERSON OR PERSONS UNKNOWN.

THREE DAYS LATER, A FUNERAL TAKES PLACE AT MOUNTAIN VIEW CEMETERY IN OAKLAND CALIFORNIA.

SIX FAMILY MEMBERS ARE IN ATTENDANCE.

SEVERAL DETECTIVES ARE ALSO ON HAND.

BUT THEY SPOT NO SUSPICIOUS CHARACTERS.

**FRIDAY, JANUARY 24**
IT COMES TO LIGHT THAT SOME OF THE DEAD WOMAN'S POSSESSIONS — SHOES AND A PURSE — HAVE BEEN FOUND.

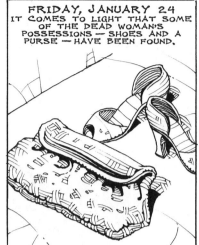

THEY WERE ORIGINALLY DISCOVERED THE DAY AFTER THE MURDER, IN A TRASH BIN BEHIND A RESTAURANT AT 1135 S. CRENSHAW BLVD...

BUT WERE TAKEN TO THE CITY DUMP AND ONLY NOW RECOVERED.

THE RESTAURANT IS LOCATED NORTH OF WHERE THE BODY WAS FOUND, THE KILLER APPARENTLY HAVING DISPOSED OF THE ARTICLES ON HIS WAY TO OR FROM THE VACANT LOT.

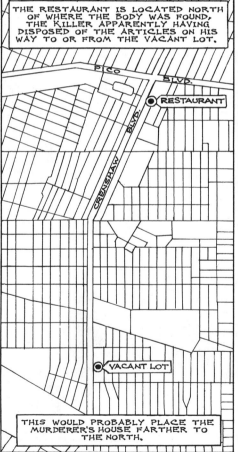

PICO BLVD.

● RESTAURANT

CRENSHAW BLVD.

● VACANT LOT

THIS WOULD PROBABLY PLACE THE MURDERER'S HOUSE FARTHER TO THE NORTH.

"RED" MANLEY IS BROUGHT IN TO IDENTIFY THE ITEMS.

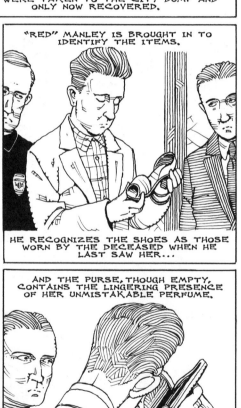

HE RECOGNIZES THE SHOES AS THOSE WORN BY THE DECEASED WHEN HE LAST SAW HER...

AND THE PURSE, THOUGH EMPTY, CONTAINS THE LINGERING PRESENCE OF HER UNMISTAKABLE PERFUME.

BY THIS TIME, WITH NO SUSPECTS AND NO NEW LEADS, THE BLACK DAHLIA INVESTIGATION FALLS FROM THE HEADLINES AND APPEARS TO LOSE STEAM.

THURSDAY, JANUARY 23
JAMES RICHARDSON, CITY EDITOR OF THE EXAMINER, RECEIVES A MYSTERIOUS PHONE CALL.

MR. RICHARDSON, I MUST CONGRATULATE YOU ON WHAT THE EXAMINER HAS DONE IN THE BLACK DAHLIA CASE.

THANK YOU.

YOU SEEM TO HAVE RUN OUT OF MATERIAL.

THAT'S RIGHT.

MAYBE I CAN BE OF ASSISTANCE.

I'LL TELL YOU WHAT I'LL DO. I'LL SEND YOU SOME OF THE THINGS SHE HAD WITH HER WHEN SHE, SHALL WE SAY, DISAPPEARED.

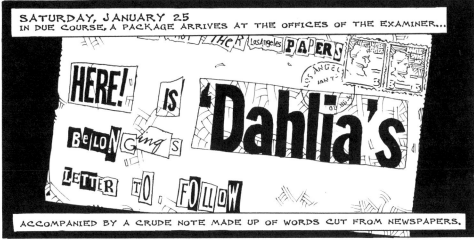

SATURDAY, JANUARY 25
IN DUE COURSE, A PACKAGE ARRIVES AT THE OFFICES OF THE EXAMINER...

HERE! IS 'Dahlia's BeLONGinGS LetTeR TO FOLLOW

ACCOMPANIED BY A CRUDE NOTE MADE UP OF WORDS CUT FROM NEWSPAPERS.

THE PACKAGE CONTAINS ELIZABETH SHORT'S BIRTH CERTIFICATE AND SOCIAL SECURITY CARD, SEVERAL PHOTOGRAPHS, BUSINESS CARDS, AND THE CLAIM CHECKS FOR THE BAGS SHE LEFT AT THE GREYHOUND DEPOT.

EVERY ITEM HAS BEEN SOAKED IN GASOLINE, TO ELIMINATE FINGERPRINTS.

IS THIS, AS SOME CYNICS CLAIM, A HOAX GENERATED BY THE EDITOR, USING POSSESSIONS FROM THE LADY'S LUGGAGE?

ALL OF THEM, HOWEVER, SEEM TO BE WHAT SHE WOULD NATURALLY HAVE CARRIED IN HER PURSE.

59

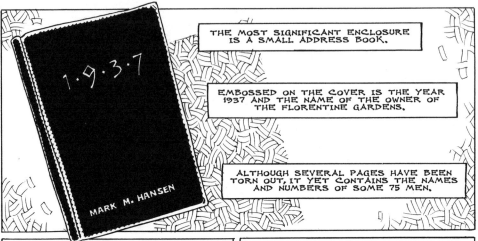

THE MOST SIGNIFICANT ENCLOSURE IS A SMALL ADDRESS BOOK.

EMBOSSED ON THE COVER IS THE YEAR 1937 AND THE NAME OF THE OWNER OF THE FLORENTINE GARDENS.

ALTHOUGH SEVERAL PAGES HAVE BEEN TORN OUT, IT YET CONTAINS THE NAMES AND NUMBERS OF SOME 75 MEN.

1·9·3·7

MARK M. HANSEN

EACH OF THEM WILL BE PAINSTAKINGLY TRACKED DOWN AND INTERVIEWED...

AND CLEARED OF ANY INVOLVEMENT.

MOST OF THEM GIVE THE SAME PORTRAIT OF THE VICTIM:

A SINGLE EVENING'S ENCOUNTER WITH DRINKS AND DINNER. SHE WAS VERY LIVELY AND AFFECTIONATE BUT WOULD NOT "PUT OUT."

MARK HANSEN IS BRIEFLY CONSIDERED A SUSPECT, BUT HE IS WELL ACCOUNTED FOR DURING THE NIGHT OF THE MURDER.

HE INSISTS THAT HE WAS NEVER INTIMATE WITH ELIZABETH SHORT.

HE FURTHER CLAIMS THAT THE ADDRESS BOOK WAS STOLEN FROM HIS OFFICE AND WAS EMPTY WHEN HE LAST SAW IT.

THIS SEEMS UNLIKELY FOR A BOOK HE HAS KEPT FOR TEN YEARS. BUT HANDWRITING ANALYSIS SHOWS THAT THE NAMES WERE ALL WRITTEN BY ELIZABETH SHORT.

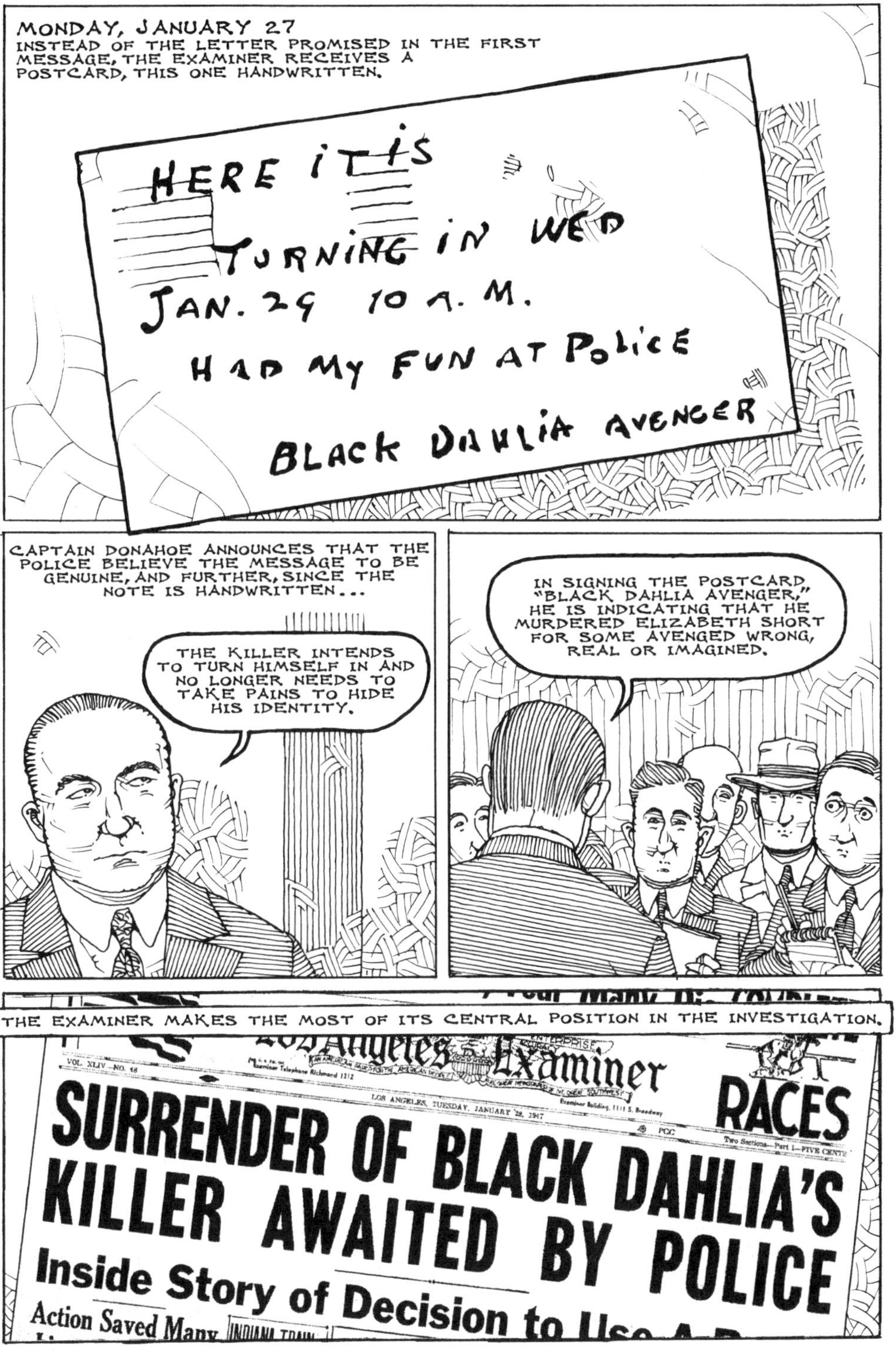
MONDAY, JANUARY 27
INSTEAD OF THE LETTER PROMISED IN THE FIRST MESSAGE, THE EXAMINER RECEIVES A POSTCARD, THIS ONE HANDWRITTEN.
HERE IT IS
TURNING IN WED
JAN. 29 10 A.M.
HAD MY FUN AT POLICE
BLACK DAHLIA AVENGER
CAPTAIN DONAHOE ANNOUNCES THAT THE POLICE BELIEVE THE MESSAGE TO BE GENUINE, AND FURTHER, SINCE THE NOTE IS HANDWRITTEN...
THE KILLER INTENDS TO TURN HIMSELF IN AND NO LONGER NEEDS TO TAKE PAINS TO HIDE HIS IDENTITY.
IN SIGNING THE POSTCARD "BLACK DAHLIA AVENGER," HE IS INDICATING THAT HE MURDERED ELIZABETH SHORT FOR SOME AVENGED WRONG, REAL OR IMAGINED.
THE EXAMINER MAKES THE MOST OF ITS CENTRAL POSITION IN THE INVESTIGATION.
Los Angeles Examiner
LOS ANGELES, TUESDAY, JANUARY 28, 1947
RACES
SURRENDER OF BLACK DAHLIA'S KILLER AWAITED BY POLICE
Inside Story of Decision to Use A...
Action Saved Many

AS IT TURNS OUT, THE KILLER DOES NOT SURRENDER.
INSTEAD, THE NEWSPAPER RECEIVES SEVERAL
MORE PASTED-UP MESSAGES.

WEDNESDAY,
JANUARY 29

Dahlia's killer cracking,
wAnts TERmS

I Will GIVE UP IN
Dahlia KILLing if I Get
10 Years
DON'T tRY TO Find Me

HAve changed my mind.
you would not give me a
square Deal. Dahlia killing
was Justified.

THURSDAY,
JANUARY 30

FROM THE EXAMINATION OF THE ENVELOPES AND PAPER
USED, THE POLICE CRIME LAB DETERMINES THAT ALL OF
THESE PASTED-UP NOTES WERE ASSEMBLED BY
THE SAME PERSON.

'Go Slow'
Tuesday January 23, 1947
MAN KILLER SAYS
Black Dahlia Case

I hAve DECided NOT To
Surrender TOO MUch
Fun Fooling POLICE

THE PERSON
SENDING THOSE
OTHER NOTES
OUGHT TO BE
ARRESTED FOR
FORGERY. HA HA!
B.D.A.

POST CARD
HEARLD
EXPRESS

OVER THE NEXT SEVERAL DAYS, MORE NOTES, SOME
HANDWRITTEN AND SIGNED "B.D.A." ARE RECEIVED BUT,
LIKE THE OTHERS, LEAD NOWHERE.

BY THIS TIME, POLICE HAVE HAD TO DEAL WITH DOZENS OF FALSE "TIPS" AND CONFESSIONS, SOME FROM AS FAR AWAY AS EL PASO AND THE BRONX.

EACH ONE MUST BE CHECKED OUT, LEADING TO MUCH WASTED TIME AND MANPOWER.

MOST OF THESE "CONFESSING SAMS" JUST WANT A MOMENT'S ATTENTION...

SUCH AS DANIEL VOORHEES, AN UNBALANCED YOUNG MAN WHO COLORFULLY DESCRIBES SLICING THE VICTIM IN HALF.

BUT NONE OF THEM CAN ANSWER THE CRUCIAL "CONTROL" QUESTION GIVEN BY INTERROGATORS—A DETAIL FROM THE AUTOPSY NEVER RELEASED TO THE PUBLIC.

IN EARLY FEBRUARY THE PAPERS ARE FILLED WITH THE STORY OF JOSEPH DUMAIS, AN ARMY CORPORAL AT FT. DIX NEW JERSEY...

WHO WROTE OUT A 50-PAGE CONFESSION THAT SEEMED QUITE CONVINCING TO MANY PEOPLE.

HE WAS BRIEFLY TAKEN INTO CUSTODY AND SOON CLEARED OF ANY INVOLVEMENT.

NEVERTHELESS, A FALSE STORY IS PLANTED BY POLICE, IN A FAILED SCHEME TO LURE THE TRUE KILLER INTO THE OPEN.

BY THIS TIME, A MERE TWO WEEKS AFTER THE DISCOVERY OF THE BODY, THE BLACK DAHLIA INVESTIGATION HAS EXHAUSTED ITS MOMENTUM. ALL AVENUES HAVE LED NOWHERE.

ON FEBRUARY 1, CAPTAIN DONAHOE MAKES AN ANNOUNCEMENT:

IT APPEARS IMPROBABLE THAT THE SHORT GIRL WAS MURDERED IN THE CITY.

IF SHE WERE, HE FEELS CERTAIN THAT THE SITE WOULD HAVE BEEN FOUND BY NOW.

AND SO THE CASE, WHILE STILL OPEN, MOVES TO INACTIVE STATUS.

# PART V

# WRAP-UP

## 1949

IN THE YEARS FOLLOWING THE BLACK DAHLIA MURDER, THE
PROBLEM OF VIOLENCE ON THE STREETS OF LOS ANGELES
REACHES THE POINT OF PUBLIC OUTRAGE.

BY THIS TIME, MANY OBSERVERS HAVE NOTED THE LONG SERIES OF UNSOLVED MURDERS OF WOMEN IN THE CITY, GOING BACK SEVERAL YEARS.

MOST, LIKE ELIZABETH SHORT, WERE UNATTACHED, LIVING ALONE, KILLED ELSEWHERE AND DUMPED NAKED IN A PUBLIC PLACE.

ORA MURRAY. AGE 42. JULY 22, 1943. THE "WHITE GARDENIA" MURDER. BEATEN TO DEATH, A FLOWER PLACED UNDER HER RIGHT SHOULDER.

GEORGETTE BAUERDORF, AGE 20. OCTOBER 12, 1944. A HOSTESS, WITH SHORT, AT THE HOLLYWOOD CANTEEN. FOUND CHOKED TO DEATH IN THE BATHTUB OF HER HOME.

JEAN FRENCH, AGE 40. FEBRUARY 10, 1947. THE "RED LIPSTICK" MURDER. FOUND SLASHED AND BLUDGEONED. THE KILLER WROTE WITH LIPSTICK ON HER NAKED BODY.

EVELYN WINTERS, AGE 42. MARCH 12, 1947. BEATEN TO DEATH.

LAURA ELIZABETH TRELSTAD,
AGE 37. MAY 11 1947.
VICTIM OF STRANGULATION,
SKULL FRACTURE.

ROSENDA MONDRAGON, AGE 20.
JULY 8, 1947.
FOUND STRANGLED AND STABBED.

VIOLA NORTON, AGE 36.
FEBRUARY 14, 1948.
BEATEN TO DEATH.

COULD ALL OF THESE ATROCITIES BE THE PRODUCT
OF THE SAME HAND? OR IS LOS ANGELES OVERRUN
BY HOMICIDAL LUNATICS?

LOUISE MARGARET SPRINGER,
AGE 28. JUNE 18 1949.
KIDNAPPED IN HER CAR, FOUND
THERE BATTERED TO DEATH.

GLADYS EUGENIA KERN, AGE 50.
FEBRUARY 16, 1948. A REAL
ESTATE AGENT, FOUND STABBED
TO DEATH IN AN EMPTY HOUSE.

ALSO DURING THESE YEARS, THE ACTIVITIES OF ORGANIZED CRIME HAVE BECOME EVER HARDER TO IGNORE.

THE DEADLY RIVALRY BETWEEN THE EAST COAST MAFIA HEADED BY JACK DRAGNA...

AND THE JEWISH UPSTART "BUGSY" SIEGEL REACHED A BOILING POINT IN JUNE, 1947...

WHEN SIEGEL WAS SHOT TO DEATH IN HIS BEVERLY HILLS HOME.

ON AUGUST 19, 1948, SIEGEL'S PARTNER, MICKEY COHEN, SURVIVES AN ASSASSINATION ATTEMPT AT HIS SUNSET STRIP HEADQUARTERS, IN WHICH ONE OF HIS HENCHMEN IS KILLED.

ANOTHER ATTEMPT COMES ON JANUARY 20, 1949, WHEN HE AND HIS PARTY ARE AMBUSHED WHILE LEAVING SHERRY'S RESTAURANT ON SUNSET BLVD.

GUNMEN FIRE FROM ACROSS THE STREET; TWO OF COHEN'S PARTY ARE KILLED, THREE WOUNDED.

IN THE MEANTIME, A NEW SUSPECT IN THE BLACK DAHLIA CASE EMERGES.

THE LAPD'S "PSYCHIATRIC CONSULTANT," PAUL DE RIVER, HAS RECEIVED A LETTER FROM A YOUNG MAN NAMED LESLIE DILLON, AGE 27, NOW WORKING AS A BELLHOP AT A FLORIDA HOTEL.

IN IT, DILLON STATES THAT HE LIVED IN LOS ANGELES AT THE TIME OF THE MURDER AND FOLLOWED THE CASE CLOSELY.

HE HAS DEVELOPED SEVERAL THEORIES OF HIS OWN. HIS KNOWLEDGE OF THE CASE IS QUITE EXTENSIVE.

IN JANUARY, 1949, CONVINCED THAT DILLON IS ACTUALLY THE KILLER, DE RIVER, WHO IS NEITHER A POLICEMAN NOR A PSYCHIATRIST, LURES HIM TO LOS ANGELES UNDER THE PRETEXT OF CONSULTING WITH HIM ABOUT THE MURDER.

INSTEAD, DILLON IS HELD INCOMMUNICADO AT A DOWNTOWN HOTEL AND PRESSURED BY POLICE TO CONFESS THE CRIME.

DURING THIS TIME, THE PRISONER MANAGES TO DROP A POSTCARD FROM THE HOTEL WINDOW...

ADDRESSED TO THE WELL-KNOWN LAWYER JERRY GIESLER.

ON JANUARY 10, DILLON IS PLACED UNDER ARREST, TAKEN TO CENTRAL HOMICIDE, PARADED BEFORE THE PRESS IN HANDCUFFS...

AND BOOKED FOR THE MURDER OF ELIZABETH SHORT.

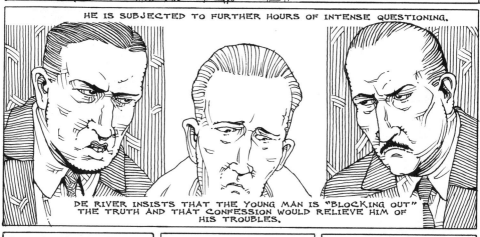

HE IS SUBJECTED TO FURTHER HOURS OF INTENSE QUESTIONING.

DE RIVER INSISTS THAT THE YOUNG MAN IS "BLOCKING OUT" THE TRUTH AND THAT CONFESSION WOULD RELIEVE HIM OF HIS TROUBLES.

SOON AFTER HIS ARREST, THOUGH, THE CASE AGAINST LESLIE DILLON FALLS APART.

EMPLOYMENT RECORDS CONFIRM THAT HE WAS AT WORK IN SAN FRANCISCO AT THE TIME OF THE MURDER.

GIESLER'S OFFICE, WHICH HAS RECEIVED THE POSTCARD, FILES A WRIT OF HABEAS CORPUS.

AND THE POLICE, WITH NO EVIDENCE TO HOLD THE YOUNG MAN, ARE FORCED TO RELEASE HIM.

IT IS A MAJOR EMBARRASSMENT FOR THE DEPARTMENT AND FURTHER FUELS THE PUBLIC OUTCRY.

THE LOS ANGELES COUNTY GRAND JURY OPENS ITS 1949 TERM IN OCTOBER...

UNDER THE SUPERVISION OF CHIEF INVESTIGATOR FRANK B. JEMISON.

HIS DEPUTY IS FINIS BROWN, A LEAD DETECTIVE IN THE BLACK DAHLIA CASE AND MEMBER OF THE LAPD'S GANGSTER SQUAD.

THE PANEL HAS A FULL AGENDA.

AMONG THE TOPICS SET FOR SCRUTINY ARE: THE "SUNSET STRIP" WARS AND THE ATTEMPTS ON THE LIFE OF MICKEY COHEN; THE SYNDICATE-RUN PROSTITUTION AND ABORTION RINGS; AND THE SEVERAL UNSOLVED MURDERS OF WOMEN OVER THE PAST DECADE, INCLUDING THAT OF ELIZABETH SHORT.

PRESUMABLY EMBEDDED IN ALL OF THESE SUBJECTS IS THE HUGE ISSUE OF POLICE CORRUPTION.

THE CHIEF OF POLICE, CLEMENCE B. HORRALL, AND HIS MEN DREAD WHAT IS COMING.

AS IT TURNS OUT, THE BLACK DAHLIA IS THE ABSOLUTE LAST SUBJECT ON THE SCHEDULE, AND, AS THE TERM COMES TO AN END, TIME IS LIMITED.

THEIR TASK IS NOT ALLEVIATED BY THE TRUNCATED LIST OF "SUSPECTS" PROVIDED BY THE POLICE—ALL OF THEM PREVIOUSLY INVESTIGATED AND EXONERATED.

THE UNFORTUNATE BELLHOP LESLIE DILLON...

THE NIGHTCLUB OWNER MARK HANSEN...

AND THE VICTIM'S OWN FATHER CLEO SHORT.

THIS LEADS TO NOT A LITTLE FRUSTRATION AMONG JURY MEMBERS.

THE LAST NAME ON THE LIST IS A NEW "PERSON OF INTEREST:" AN EX-CONVICT NAMED HENRY HUBER HOFFMAN.

72

AT THE TIME OF THE BLACK DAHLIA MURDER, HOFFMAN MANAGED A MOTEL ON FLOWER STREET...

A MERE 15-MINUTE DRIVE FROM THE VACANT LOT WHERE THE BODY WAS FOUND.

THE ACCUSATION ORIGINATED WITH THE MAN'S EX-WIFE, CLARA.

AROUND THAT TIME, SHE SAYS, SHE PEERED INTO THE UNOCCUPIED UNIT 9.

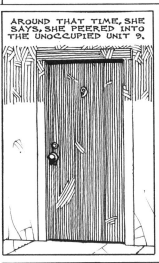

THERE, SHE FOUND A PILE OF BLOODY CLOTHING, AS WELL AS BLOOD ON THE FLOOR AND ON THE MATTRESS.

BUT THE CASE COLLAPSES WHEN THE EX-WIFE PROVES TO BE A LESS THAN RELIABLE WITNESS.

HER STORY KEEPS CHANGING.

IN ADDITION, HOFFMAN EASILY PASSES A LIE DETECTOR TEST.

AS ALL OF THESE "PRIME" SUSPECTS ARE DISMISSED BY THE GRAND JURY, THE SUSPICION ARISES THAT THE INVESTIGATION IS BEING DEFLECTED.   BUT BY NOW IT IS TOO LATE.

THE GRAND JURY TERM ENDS ON DECEMBER 29 WITH THE PANEL HAVING ISSUED NO INDICTMENTS.

THE JURORS FEEL ESPECIALLY HINDERED IN THEIR PURSUIT OF THE BLACK DAHLIA CASE: THERE WAS NO TIME TO CONDUCT A THOROUGH INQUIRY...

GRAND JURY
ROOM 546
→

AND THEY FEEL MISLED AND THWARTED IN WHAT BRIEF INQUIRY THEY DID CONDUCT.

THEIR SCATHING REPORT CITES A POLICE "CULTURE OF CORRUPTION:"

"THIS JURY HAS OBSERVED INDICATIONS OF PAYOFFS IN CONNECTION WITH PROTECTION OF VICE AND CRIME, AND GROSS MISCONDUCT ON THE PART OF SOME LAW ENFORCEMENT OFFICERS."

AS FOR THE BLACK DAHLIA CASE IN PARTICULAR:

"TESTIMONY GIVEN BY CERTAIN INVESTIGATION OFFICERS WORKING THIS CASE WAS CLEAR AND WELL DEFINED, WHILE OTHER OFFICERS SHOWED APPARENT EVASIVENESS."

THE REPORT CONCLUDES WITH THE EMPHATIC BELIEF THAT A "COVER-UP" HAS TAKEN PLACE.

DESPITE A STRONG RECOMMENDATION BY THE 1949 PANEL, THE DAHLIA INQUIRY WILL NOT BE TAKEN UP BY THE 1950 GRAND JURY.

ONE THEORY ACTIVE IN MANY QUARTERS IS THAT ELIZABETH SHORT RAN AFOUL OF CERTAIN MOBSTERS UNDER OFFICIAL PROTECTION...

WHOM SHE HAD UNDOUBTEDLY MET AMONG THE SOCIETY AT THE FLORENTINE GARDENS.

AT SOME POINT, THE STORY GOES, SHE BECAME PREGNANT...

AND FLED TO SAN DIEGO.

UPON HER RETURN, SHE SOUGHT A SOLUTION FROM THE MOB-RUN ABORTION RING...

BUT FOR SOME REASON SHE NEEDED TO BE PERMANENTLY SILENCED.

"BUGSY" SIEGEL AMONG OTHERS WAS KNOWN TO MUTILATE HIS ENEMIES.

THE SLASHED MOUTH IS A DEFINITE SICILIAN TOUCH: THE SIGN OF THE INFORMER.

AND IT WAS CERTAINLY NO ACCIDENT THAT THE VACANT LOT WHERE THE BODY WAS DUMPED IS A MERE THREE BLOCKS FROM THE HOME OF THE MAFIA CHIEF JACK DRAGNA.

OTHER OBSERVERS COUNTER THAT THE EXTREME MUTILATIONS GO FAR BEYOND A SIMPLE MOB "HIT."

THEY POINT TO A MUCH DEEPER PSYCHOPATHOLOGY.

THE FINDINGS OF THE GRAND JURY BRING ABOUT A MASSIVE SHAKE-UP WITHIN THE LAPD.

CHIEF HORRALL IS FOUND TO BE THE PRIME FACILITATOR OF THE UNDERWORLD'S INFILTRATION OF THE DEPARTMENT.

CHIEF OF POLICE

➡ 547

HE RESIGNS IN AUGUST, 1949.

GOVERNOR EARL WARREN APPOINTS THE CALIFORNIA CRIME COMMISSION.

ITS TASK: TO ROOT OUT THE INFLUENCE OF ORGANIZED CRIME IN THE ENTIRE STATE.

IN AUGUST, 1950, A NEW CHIEF, WILLIAM H. PARKER, IS APPOINTED...

AN AMBITIOUS, REFORM-MINDED VETERAN OFFICER.

HE RIDS THE DEPARTMENT OF ITS MOST EGREGIOUS CRIMINAL CONNECTIONS...

AND GENERALLY POLISHES ITS PUBLIC IMAGE.

CAPTAIN JACK DONAHOE IS FORCED TO RESIGN.

IT TURNS OUT HE WAS A MAJOR PARTICIPANT IN THE MAFIA'S DRUG RING.

OVER THE ENSUING YEARS, THE BLACK DAHLIA CASE REMAINS IN THE DEPARTMENT'S "OPEN/UNSOLVED" FILE, GROWING COLDER BY THE DAY.

HARRY HANSEN IS STILL IN CHARGE, FIELDING TIPS AND RUMORS UNTIL HIS RETIREMENT IN 1968.

IN 1981, A NEW SUSPECT EMERGES...

IN THE PERSON OF A SHADY CHARACTER CALLING HIMSELF ARNOLD SMITH.

IN A SERIES OF MEETINGS IN DOWNTOWN BARS WITH A FREELANCE WRITER NAMED JOHN GILMORE, SMITH TELLS THE STORY AS IT WAS TOLD TO HIM.

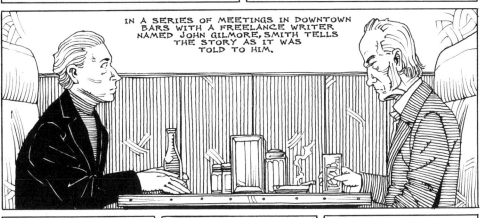

A FRIEND OF HIS NAMED "AL MORRISON" TORTURED, MURDERED AND MUTILATED ELIZABETH SHORT...

DURING A LONG NIGHT AT A HOUSE IN HOLLYWOOD.

THE ACCOUNT IS FILLED WITH SUCH DETAIL THAT GILMORE BEGINS TO SUSPECT THAT SMITH WAS ACTUALLY THERE...

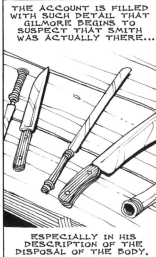

ESPECIALLY IN HIS DESCRIPTION OF THE DISPOSAL OF THE BODY.

CUTTING THE VICTIM IN HALF WAS DONE ONLY FOR EASIER TRANSPORT

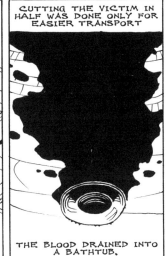

THE BLOOD DRAINED INTO A BATHTUB.

AT THIS TIME THE OFFICER IN CHARGE OF THE CASE IS DETECTIVE JOHN ST. JOHN...

KNOWN, FOR HIS DEDUCTIVE SKILLS, AS "JIGSAW JOHN."

UPON HEARING GILMORE'S STORY, HE TRACKS DOWN THE IDENTITY OF "ARNOLD SMITH"...

AN ALIAS FOR JACK ANDERSON WILSON, AGE 61, A LOCAL PETTY CRIMINAL WITH AN ARREST RECORD GOING BACK DECADES.

FURTHER, HE SURMISES THAT "AL MORRISON" IS A FICTITIOUS COVER

AND THAT WILSON IS, IN FACT, THE MURDERER.

ANOTHER MEETING WITH SMITH IS ARRANGED AT A DOWNTOWN BAR.

THIS TIME, GILMORE IS ACCOMPANIED BY AN UNDERCOVER AGENT CARRYING A CONCEALED RECORDER.

THESE TRANSCRIPTS, ALONG WITH THE WRITER'S NOTES, CONVINCE ST. JOHN THAT WILSON IS NOW THEIR PRIME SUSPECT.

AN ARREST IS IMMINENT.

THE TROUBLE IS THAT GILMORE HAS NO WAY TO FIND THE MAN.

THEIR MEETINGS COME ENTIRELY AT THE CRIMINAL'S DISCRETION: WHENEVER HE NEEDS CASH OR A FREE DRINK.

SOMEHOW, THE STORY LEAKS TO THE HERALD EXAMINER.

THEIR ISSUE OF JANUARY 17, 1982 TELLS OF A "HOT NEW SUSPECT."

BEFORE ANOTHER MEETING CAN BE ARRANGED, WILSON PERISHES IN A MYSTERIOUS FIRE IN HIS ROOM AT THE HOLLAND HOTEL.

HIS IS THE ONLY ROOM TO SUFFER ANY DAMAGE. THE ORIGIN OF THE FIRE CANNOT BE DETERMINED.

THUS ENDS THE FINAL LEAD IN THE MYSTERY OF THE BLACK DAHLIA.

TO THIS DAY, THE LAPD'S COPIOUS FILES HAVE NOT BEEN MADE PUBLIC.

OVER THE YEARS, THE STORY OF ELIZABETH SHORT CONTINUES TO FASCINATE, HORRIFY, AND INSPIRE.

A YOUNG WOMAN OF MANY FACETS:

AN AMBITIOUS STRIVER, SET ON A CAREER IN SHOW BUSINESS... AND A SUBMISSIVE INNOCENT, WHO ONLY WANTED TO MARRY A SOLDIER, SETTLE DOWN, AND RAISE A FAMILY.

AN OPEN, FRIENDLY SOCIAL BUTTERFLY... AND A MOROSE LONER, FULL OF SECRETS.

A HARD-NOSED, STREETWISE SEDUCTRESS...

AND THE PERFECT VICTIM.

ES

DAUGHTER
ELIZABETH SHORT
JULY 29, 1924 — JAN. 15, 1947

HER MODEST GRAVE CAN BE VISITED TODAY AT THE MOUNTAIN VIEW CEMETERY IN OAKLAND, CALIFORNIA.